IDIOT'S

GUIDE TO

Horoscopes

by Madeline Gerwick-Brodeur
and Lisa Lenard

alpha
books

Macmillan General Reference
1633 Broadway, New York NY 10019-6785

©1999 by Amaranth

THE POCKET IDIOT'S GUIDE name and design are trademarks of Macmillan, Inc.

Macmillan Publishing books may be purchased for business or sales promotional use. For information please write: Special Markets Department, Macmillan Publishing USA, 1633 Broadway, New York, NY 10019.

International Standard Book Number: ISBN 0-02-862702-4
Library of Congress Catalog Card Number: 98-89574

01   00 99   8 7 6 5 4 3 2 1

Interpretation of the printing code: the rightmost number of the first series of numbers is the year of the book's printing; the rightmost number of the second series of numbers is the number of the book's printing. For example, a printing code of 99-1 shows that the first printing occurred in 1999.

Printed in the United States of America

Note: This publication contains the opinions and ideas of its authors. It is intended to provide helpful and informative material on the subject matter covered. It is sold with the understanding that the authors and publisher are not engaged in rendering professional services in the book. If the reader requires personal assistance or advice, a competent professional should be consulted.

Book Producer

Amaranth

Alpha Development Team

Publisher

Kathy Nebenhaus

Editorial Director

Gary M. Krebs

Managing Editor

Bob Shuman

Marketing Brand Manager

Felice Primeau

Editor

Jessica Faust

Development Editors

Phil Kitchel
Amy Zavatto

Production Team

Development Editor

Lee Ann Chearney/Amaranth

Production Editor

Kristi Hart

Cover Designer

Mike Freeland

Photo Editor

Richard H. Fox

Illustrator

Jody P. Schaeffer

Book Designers

Scott Cook and Amy Adams of DesignLab

Indexer

Greg Pearson

Layout/Proofreading

Angela Calvert
Mary Hunt

Contents

Introduction

Okay, so you're probably familiar with Sun sign forecasts, those horoscopes that appear in the daily newspapers. And you probably know your Sun sign, too. But did you know that the Sun signs are just the beginning of astrology? Did you know, for example, that all 12 signs appear somewhere in your birth chart? Or that, in addition to the Sun, the Moon and planets appear in your birth chart, too? Do you know what your ascendant is, the sign that has just risen over the horizon at the moment of your birth? Your ascendant, or rising sign, represents the "you" that the outside world perceives, as well as personality traits, needs, and your physical characteristics.

There's much more to astrology, and *you*, than your Sun sign! This book will help you:

➤ Discover the true nature of Sun sign personalities

➤ Find your rising sign and discover what it means about how you interact with the world at large

➤ Navigate birth chart basics

➤ Learn about the role of the planets and the houses

➤ Understand astrological trends and cycles, such as retrogrades

➤ See what's coming up for the year 2000 and the 21st century!

There are probably as many maps to the human psyche as there are humans, but astrology introduces you to the oldest of them all. Astrology is an ancient science, but it's also the newest, constantly evolving along with humankind. Today, in fact, more people rely on astrology than any other method for understanding themselves and their relationships. So, enjoy your own personal exploration of the heavens and your unique place in the universe, via the study of astrology!

Extras

This no-nonsense book will guide you through the complexities of astrology. In addition to helping you understand and learn more about the Sun signs and astrology, you'll find helpful boxes throughout the book that provide you with extra information to help make that journey even easier. Here's what each box contains:

Written in the Skies

These astrological tips are just the tip of the iceberg to all that the heavens hold written in the skies!

Out of Orbit

Take care with these cautionary sidebars; they can help you avoid going out of sync with the universe.

Star Words

These sidebars define astrological terms so that you, too, can speak the universal language of the heavens.

Trademarks

All terms mentioned in this book that are known to be or are suspected of being trademarks or service marks have been appropriately capitalized. Alpha books and Macmillan General Reference cannot attest to the accuracy of this information. Use of a term in this book should not be regarded as affecting the validity of any trademark or service mark.

Chapter 1

So What's the Big Deal About Astrology, Anyway?

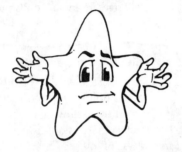

In the Beginning

Long before physics, chemistry, biology, or any of those other subjects you tried to avoid in high school or college, there was astrology. Astrology, in fact, was the first science. As early as 2900 B.C., the Sumerians built temples in the form of ziggurats, or terraced pyramids, to observe the stars and planets. It's a pretty safe assumption that astrology existed even prior to this. Astrology began as the study of the "wandering" stars, or planets, as we know them today. It's actually the study of cycles indicated by planetary movements, and associated with energies and events occurring at the same time on Earth. It uses the harmony of the universe to observe the possibilities of human behavior and experience. Astrologers analyze the position of the planets at the time and place you were born to map your strengths and challenges and your soul's purpose.

Written in the Skies

Astrology studies how your birth chart or horoscope represents your possibilities: knowing if you have a tendency to be direct in matters of business or circumspect in matters of love, for example, can help you determine how to use such strengths and weaknesses to your best advantage. Think of astrology as a way of discovering more about your unique self.

Your birth chart or horoscope is a unique map of who you are. Using the date, time, and place of your birth, it shows the positions of the planets in the signs and houses. The odds of anyone else having exactly the same horoscope as you are astronomically small. From it's humble beginnings, astrology soon developed into an incredibly complex practice. By 2000 B.C., the magi of Mesopotamia believed that there were no accidents, and that everything in the universe—people, objects, and events—was connected. Not only did the magi (priests trained in astrology and other sacred knowledge) study the stars, they looked for omens in the weather, predicted the future from the livers and intestines of animals, and listened to what they believed to be the words of trees, dogs, cats, and insects to hear what they had to say.

All About Relationships, Planetary, That Is

Let's forget about the magi for the time being and picture our ancestors, standing outside, looking up. What did they see? Well, they saw what we see: stars, and planets, and meteors. They saw the Milky Way, and the sunrise and the sunset, and the Moon in all its phases. Long before other sciences came along, in fact, astrology was used to explore the relationship between the position of Earth and the positions of those bodies in the heavens. In ancient times, astrology and astronomy were one science, and astrologers were the best-educated people: they had to understand astronomy, math, spiritual symbols and mystic meanings, psychology, and human nature. It shouldn't come as a surprise, then, that astrology was taught in the universities until the 1600s, when "rational science" took over. Today, most astrologers are still very well-educated and often hold college degrees in various fields. They frequently have training in psychology or counseling, and in addition to their in-depth knowledge of astrology have a great deal of spiritual understanding.

Put simply, astrology is based on the relationships between the *planets*; the Sun and the Moon; 12 *zodiac*, or Sun, *signs*; and 12 areas of a person's life, called *houses*. Even after thousands of years, astrology is still the most complex psychological model available, offering explanations for phenomena rational science just can't address.

Star Words

Planets represent the various energies of a person, as manifested in each *house*. The *zodiac* is the name of the elliptical pattern the Earth follows in its annual revolution around the Sun, passing through each of the 12 astrological *signs*.

Planets are the "what" of astrology. They represent your various energies, including your mental and emotional nature, desires, vitality, soul, will, consciousness, and sub-conscious, as well as the people in your life. Throughout this book, we'll be including the Sun and Moon, even though they aren't actually planets. The zodiac is the name of the elliptic pattern the Earth follows in its annual revolution around the Sun. This path is always the same, and always passes through the same 12 signs: Aries ♈, Taurus ♉, Gemini ♊, Cancer ♋, Leo ♌, Virgo ♍, Libra ♎, Scorpio ♏, Sagittarius ♐, Capricorn ♑, Aquarius ♒, and Pisces ♓. All zodiac signs appear in everyone's chart. Signs are the "how" of astrology, and show the needs and styles of the planets, as well as what methods could be used to achieve them. The houses are the "where" of astrology. Each of the 12 houses encompasses a specific arena of life and is the stage where the drama of the planets unfolds. And you thought astrology was for idiots!

The Calendar and Astrology

You probably didn't know that all common calendar cycles are reflected by the movement in the heavens—and in astrology. A month, for example, is roughly the amount of time between New Moons (about 29 days). And, coincidentally, a month is approximately the amount of time it takes for the Sun to move to a new sign in the zodiac. A year is the amount of time the ancients thought it took for the Sun to travel through the entire zodiac (from the perspective of Earth), but today we know it's the time it takes the earth to travel around the Sun. (Still, pretty smart for a bunch of guys without comput-ers!) These same smart guys noticed that the Sun was moving through certain constellations at certain times of the year. Each constellation had a specific meaning for the ancients, a meaning reflected when the 12 zodiac signs were named. A week, as you know, has seven days, but you may not have known that's because that's how many planets could be seen by the ancients. In fact, the days of the week are named after the Sun, the Moon and the first five planets, not including the Earth:

Sunday	Sun
Monday	Moon
Tuesday (*mardi* in French)	Mars
Wednesday (*mercredi* in French)	Mercury
Thursday (*jeudi* in French)	Jupiter
Friday (*vendredi* in French)	Venus
Saturday	Saturn

Sunday   Monday   Tuesday

Wednesday   Thursday   Friday   Saturday

The days are named for the first seven discovered celestial bodies, not including the Earth.

Let's Get Rid of Some Myths About Astrology

We modern types like to think that we "know better" than to believe in astrology, but much of what we think we know about astrology is actually not true at all. For example, astrologers never say that the planets influence human behavior, and, not only is astrology not a "dark art," many smart people, including some well-known physicists, use astrology's ideas as the basis for some far more complex scientific theories. So let's debunk some of those myths about astrology.

Do the Planets Make You Do Things?

The planets do not cause things to happen, or make people behave in certain ways. Actually, the planets are like barometers, or indicators of the same energies occurring on Earth—in people, in places, in everything. We can watch the planets and use them as coincident indicators of what's happening here, or in a person or place, for example. But to attribute cause or influence to the planets is like attributing the outside temperature to a thermometer. No one would do that! Astrology is a symbolic system that appears to work via *synchronicity*, sometimes known as meaningful coincidences, an idea first proposed by psychoanalysis pioneer Carl Jung. In terms of astrology, this means that what occurs overhead is merely a reflection of what is happening on Earth. In other words, the two are coincident with each other, or synchronous.

Star Words

Synchronicity is (in addition to being the name of one of the Police's albums) the idea that everything in the universe is interconnected, a pattern of meaningful coincidences—or, as Jung said, everything that is born or occurs at a particular time has the energies of that time!

Astrology Is Not Black Magic or Voodoo

Okay, then how does astrology work? Astrology is based on three spiritual premises:

➤ The outer reflects the inner, or, our external lives actually reflect what is happening internally.

➤ A person's chart shows his or her soul's purpose.

➤ Each person is continually evolving spiritually.

The Bible is actually filled with astrological information and messages, but without training no one would ever know it. For example, the 12 disciples of Christ and the 12 tribes or houses of Israel each represented one of the 12 zodiac signs. Christ ushered in the Piscean Age, and the symbol of the fish (Pisces is symbolized by fish) was used as the secret symbol of Christians. The mystical Jewish text, the Kabbalah, has mystical and astrological meanings as well. One book, for example, the Zohar, describes God as containing all of life—and each life containing all of God. And, according to the Zohar, an astrological chart was considered an expression of the Divine Will of God.

Astrologers and Scientists Have a Lot in Common

Some physicists now believe that astrology shows the order underneath what we see on the surface. This theory is based on physicist David Bohm's work (Bohm was one of Einstein's right-hand men). Basically, Bohm explains how energy, matter, and meaning are enfolded together, and he has written formulas that support this, kind of like $E=mc^2$. Bohm's theory explains how inner and outer reality is interwoven, or, as physicist Will Keepin puts it, "The nature of reality is a single undivided wholeness." In other words, we are all part of something, and, like DNA, we each contain the pattern of that something as well. Keepin explains that for each point in space-time, a unique astrological chart exists. Or, to put it another way, when astrologers define an astrological chart, they need a specific point in space plus a specific point in time—and that point is you! You don't get much more scientific than that!

Just a Few of the Smart Folks Who Use Astrology

Carl Jung not only recognized the synchronicity that is the basis of astrology, he once said, "We are born at a given moment, in a given place, and like vintage years of wine, we have the qualities of the year and of the season in which we are born." T. S. Eliot's epic poem "The Waste Land" is filled with astrological references, and four of its sections are named for the astrological *elements*: fire, earth, air, and water.

Star Words

The four *elements* describe the basic qualities of the signs and of life. There are three signs for each element: The fire signs are Aries, Leo, and Sagittarius; the earth signs are Taurus, Virgo, and Capricorn; the air signs are Gemini, Libra, and Aquarius; and the water signs are Cancer, Scorpio, and Pisces.

Another well-known user of astrology is Nancy Reagan, who, after the assassination attempt on her husband Ronald Reagan in 1981, used astrology to determine the best times and worst times for Reagan to do everything from sign bills to travel to foreign countries. While the news media made fun of Mrs. Reagan at the time, it should be noted that Reagan was the first president since Jefferson elected in a year ending in "0" not to die in office. Using astrology can't hurt. Many other smart people

have used astrology, including turn-of-the-century financier J. P. Morgan, who used astrology for business timing
to amass his fortune. Morgan may have summed it up
best when he said, "Millionaires don't use astrology; bil-
lionaires do."

Name-Dropping: Some Astrologers You May Have Heard Of

Smart people have been using astrology since astrology
began, and in fact, there are a lot of historical folks who
were astrologers. Here are some examples.

The Three Wise Men

Have you ever wondered why the Three Wise Men were
looking for that star over Bethlehem in the first place?
Well, it was because they were astrologers. It is believed
that they learned from studying the stars that the Christ
child would be born at the time of a conjunction of planets that signaled the arrival of a new age (the Piscean).
Still, it wasn't quite as easy at it sounds: the two planets—
Jupiter and Saturn—were bright, but not something an av-
erage person would have noticed. Even though they were
trained astrologers, it took them some time to actually lo-
cate Jesus in Bethlehem. But if they hadn't studied the
stars, they might not have been looking in the first place!

Written in the Skies

A conjunction of planets occurs
when the two planets appear in the
same place in the sky at the same
time. It signifies the beginning of a
new cycle, a cycle that reflects the energies of the
planets involved.

Pythagoras (580?–500? B.C.)

So maybe you can't remember the Pythagorean theorem (try to remember the Scarecrow reciting it in The Wizard of Oz—something about the hypotenuse of a right triangle). It may surprise you to learn that the mathematician responsible for that leap of logic was also an astrologer. In addition to the Pythagorean theorem, Pythagoras also gave us the musical scale, and he believed that, similar to musical harmonies, the larger harmony of the universe could be discovered in numbers as well. (It is still believed by many mathematicians that the secret of the universe can be discovered somewhere in pi, the ratio of a circle's circumference to its diameter.)

Nostradamus (1503–1566)

This is the guy who predicted most of the bad stuff that's happened this century, like world wars, atomic bombs, and assassinations. Nostradamus's predictions, written in 1555, foretold everything that would happen from that date until the end of the world, which he posted at 3797 A.D. (Thank goodness!). What did he base those predictions on? You guessed it: astrology. Nostradamus predicted many disasters and tough times, but he predicted some good stuff, too, including a Golden Age, or 1,000 years of peace, at the millennium (let's hope he's right!). After all, in addition to being an astrologer and a seer, Nostradamus was also a practicing physician, so his motto was "Do no harm."

Isaac Newton (1642–1727)

Long before he sat under the proverbial apple tree, Isaac Newton was a practicing astrologer. Like all 16th-century scientists, he studied the stars, and understood the larger relationship between everything that's since been largely ignored by the rational sciences. Among Newton's many ponderings were questions about the secret of the universe, the nature of gravity itself (yes, it exists—but why?), and a belief in the existence of animal spirits in the human body. It's ironic that scientists after Newton would use Newton's Laws to discount any further examination of the more occult sciences he himself had examined!

How You Can Steer by the Stars

Well, we all know the ancient navigators thought the world was flat, and yet they got into those ships of theirs anyway. How did they steer? Remember, this is before radar and sonar and cell phones (which is probably why it took Odysseus so long to return home after the Trojan War). You guessed it again: they steered by the stars. Ancient astrologers drew maps of the sky, and, just as we notice the sun rising and setting in slightly different places at different times of year, those maps showed where certain constellations would be at certain times of year. This was called celestial navigation: those ancient ship captains could just point toward Orion and sail toward Cairo (or wherever it was they wanted to go). And while celestial navigation, the most ancient way to plot a course, can be limited by the weather (you can't see the stars if it's cloudy, after all), it is still used today.

Out of Orbit

It's popular to assume that astrology is the same as fate. Not so! Astrology shows potentials, just as a map can show you possible routes. But to think of astrology as an absolute is a big mistake. Instead of looking to astrology for answers, look at it for choices. You provide the answers—you pick the route you want to take.

But the stars were used for more than navigation: they also were used to help determine when to sow and when to reap, and they reminded people when to celebrate various holidays. The ancient people noticed that there was a regularity to the movements of the planets, and that everything from the seasons to social needs could be predicted by those patterns. Astrology is a symbolic system from which we can learn the interconnection between external reality and internal reality. Like the smart people we've learned about, we can use astrology as a map for our own route through life. Like those ancient sailors, we, too, can learn to steer by the stars!

Chapter 2

What Astrology Can Reveal in Your Everyday Life

In This Chapter

➤ Your horoscope and your love life

➤ Your horoscope and your job

➤ Your horoscope and your health

➤ Your horoscope and your money

➤ Your horoscope and where you live

Astrologers Are Specialists, Too

Just like doctors, lawyers, or teachers, astrologers have different areas of expertise, based on their backgrounds and interests. Astrology is used in many different ways, from counseling kings and business leaders about strategies, tactics, and timing to learning about personal astrology for health, vocation, relationships, evolutionary paths, strengths, and challenges.

There are astrologers who specialize in the stock market, in business, or in sports. And there are those who specialize in psychological astrology, which gets to the root of why you behave a certain way and explores your mental makeup. So, move over brokers, bankers, personal trainers, and therapists—make room for astrologers!

Out of Orbit

Astrological charts can be interpreted and understood on many different levels. The same astrological symbol can represent events in your childhood, people in your life, an internalized psychological complex, or a spiritual lesson. Don't assume that if you know one possible interpretation for a particular item, you understand it completely.

In addition to helping you understand various areas of your life, astrology also can predict what you might do next. Part of this stems from the fact that people don't change their behavior very much—predicting that Liz Taylor might get married again may not be a great stretch—but because there are actually many different ways the same energy or prediction can manifest itself, predictions don't limit your scope, but rather, show your direction. Hey, Liz, maybe another marriage isn't the answer...

It's also important to remember that the "outer" reflects the "inner," so if you're in complete inner turmoil, that's what's going to manifest itself, not what you want to control and have happen. We all know someone who always seems to pick the wrong guy or gal—that's an example of what we mean here.

You do have more control than you realize, but much of it is given over to your subconscious, and so may manifest itself as your fears—or as a replaying of scenes from your childhood to discredit something you learned then. You may try to run, but you can't hide from yourself.

How much conscious control you have usually depends on how aware you become of your own issues and strengths. Still, what happens is entirely up to you—and what you do with your potential.

Your Horoscope and Your Love Life

Your relationships are based on all the planets, signs, and houses in your birth chart—and how they interact with all the planets, signs, and houses in other people's charts. (And here you thought it was that great new hairstyle.) *Relationship astrology* studies just how compatible two (or more) people are, taking into account all the different aspects between the people, as well as what type of relationship it is.

Star Words

Relationship astrology studies people's charts to determine their compatibility—or incompatibility.

Relationship astrology can tell whether two people are emotionally, mentally, or sexually compatible, and whether they would work well together as partners, as boss and employee, "just be good friends,"—or recommend they avoid each other like the plague. And while you can't choose your family, with relationship astrology, at least you'll have fun exploring your family's dys"fun"ction. Who knows, maybe you'll gain some valuable insights.

Relationship astrology also can tell you when one person in a relationship will want to control the other one and in what ways—devious, bold, good-intentioned, steam rolling, empowered, manipulative, unconscious—the assault will be launched. Relationship astrology can determine if you have similar or conflicting value systems or beliefs, as well as many other specific issues and strengths. Relationship astrology, in other words, can save you a whole lot of heartache and headaches right from the start. In some countries where marriages are arranged, remember, astrologers are consulted first to determine if two people are compatible. Only then is the couple approved for marriage by the families. So consider yourself lucky that you get to choose for yourself!

Your Horoscope and Your Career

Vocational astrology assesses your various personality traits and needs, your productive resources and capabilities, your special talents, and the paths you have taken up to now, as well as what type of work you will find rewarding in order to recommend the best possibilities for your career. Imagine—all this, just from carefully studying your birth chart.

Star Words

Vocational astrology studies your potentials in order to determine your career or path.

What kind of work you will do is related to your Sun sign—but it's not quite that simple. Let's use the example of a Gemini Sun sign, which signals work in communications. You might be a journalist or teacher, a writer, someone who creates Web sites, or you might work in advertising. Maybe you'll be a manager, negotiate contracts, or work as a partner in a business.

Or, you might travel or work with foreign trade, work in publishing, the legal system, or teach at a university. There's obviously a great deal more to choosing your vocation or career than just what your Sun sign can predict.

All of these examples deal with communications in some way, right? But they're all very different ways of working in communications. Vocational astrologers never look at just your Sun sign—and neither should you.

Your Horoscope and Your Health

Nothing is more important to us than our health; without it, we can't do any of the other things that matter so much to our lives—from love to work to where we live. And astrology and health have been connected for a very long time. Hippocrates, the Greek philosopher and physician who lived around 400 B.C., and who is considered the father of modern medicine (do the words "Hippocratic Oath" ring a bell?), once said, "A physician without a knowledge of astrology has no right to call himself a physician."

In "the good old days," when people went to the doctor, the first thing that doctor did was draw up their astrological charts. These days, most doctors don't do that, but we can still use what astrology can tell us to stay healthy and achieve a sense of well being.

Today, there are *medical astrologers*—and even physicians—who use astrology to discover what isn't always found through the tests commonly used in traditional medicine. Medical astrology also can be used for more basic information, like understanding your metabolic nature, the types of foods that will be helpful or stressful to you, and general areas that need to be monitored in order for you to maintain your optimum health.

Each sign of the zodiac is associated with a particular part of the body and with certain glands, and so has particular dietary and vitamin needs associated with it. Certain foods may be very good for you—and others may send you spinning. Capricorn, for example, represents the bones, joints, knees, and teeth, so naturally, a lot of protein and calcium are going to be useful if you were born under this Sun sign.

The Signs and Their Associated Parts of the Body

Sign	Associated Body Parts
Aries	Head and face
Taurus	Neck and throat
Gemini	Head, arms, shoulders, nervous system, and lungs
Cancer	Stomach and breasts
Leo	Back, spine, and heart
Virgo	Intestines, liver, pancreas, gall bladder, and bowels
Libra	Kidneys, lower back, and adrenal glands
Scorpio	Genitals, urinary and reproductive organs
Sagittarius	Liver, hips, and thighs
Capricorn	Bones, teeth, joints, and knees
Aquarius	Ankles and circulation
Pisces	Feet, immune and hormonal systems

Star Words

Medical astrology uses your chart to determine the best ways for you to stay healthy and to achieve a sense of well-being. It also can be used for diagnosis.

Like all of astrology, the connections between the signs and parts of the body are part of the science that holds that the entire cosmos is reflected in the human body. As Shakespeare's Hamlet muses, "What a piece of work is man." Remember, too, that all of the zodiac signs—not just the Sun sign you are born under—are represented in your astrological chart, and all have a bearing on a healthy you.

Your Horoscope and Your Money

Did you ever think that what you do with your money reveals a great deal about how you feel about yourself? In some signs, people may equate themselves with what they own, while others may see money as a means to an end. You may be Scrooge, Rockefeller, or Mother Teresa. As with all astrological possibilities, remember that there's nothing wrong with your personal style. For those who truly feel their home or financial status reflects themselves, it does, just as there are people who simply don't worry about money at all.

The natives of each sign handle their money in different ways: Cancers, for example, tend to hoard their cash, saving it for an unspecified rainy day; while Sagittarians may spend it freely, enjoying what's happening right this very minute.

But there are other factors at play in cosmic investment, too, and this is where *financial astrology* comes into play. Financial astrologers study the cycles of planets to determine the best available investment strategies. And they study the cycles of companies, too—so they'll know which ones are on their way up and which ones aren't. Does your mutual fund have a financial astrologer on the board?

Star Words

Financial astrology studies how and when you can best invest your money, as well as the best companies for you to invest in.

Companies have charts just like people, based on when they were incorporated or started. When these companies have certain positive astrological connections, then their stock goes up. Financial astrologers specialize in investments and the financial markets; many of them put out newsletters to help their clients become successful in the markets. (Let's get a subscription for Alan Greenspan.)

Astrology also can help determine if you're under good or challenging cycles for financial investments. If you're investing during periods when your financial cycles are challenging, there's a greater likelihood you're going to lose money, or, at best, not make any.

J. Pierpont Morgan, a very wealthy American financier at the turn of the century, used astrology for business timing purposes. He financed such companies as U.S. Steel Corporation and the Great Northern & Pacific Railroad, as well as other ventures—such as the Boer War in South Africa. His use of astrology for business investments made him a billionaire, back in the early part of this century when even a million dollars was a vast fortune.

Your Horoscope and Where You Live

Another branch of astrology can actually determine what kinds of experiences you will have in a particular location in the country or world. One type of astrology in this branch is known as relocation astrology, in which your birth chart is done for the same time and day of birth, but for a location other than your birthplace. So, your chart changes to show what your life would be like in that location. Hmm—Australia? Tahiti? Paris?

Then there's AstroCartoGraphy®. As you might suspect from its name, this type is basically a map of the world with lines all over it, showing where in the world your planets were rising and setting at the moment of your birth. (If I was born in New Jersey, then why am I strangely drawn to India?) In the place where you are now, you may feel insecure and rarely voice your feelings, but if you moved to a different location, you might be very different; your personality might blossom, and you might be positive and direct instead.

Relocation astrology can help you to determine in advance what types of experiences you might tend to have in particular places. And, depending on the location, you might have very good career circumstances, a wonderful home life, or transformational experiences that totally change your identity—or you could have more challenges than you ever dreamed of.

Addicted to Horoscopes

Do you read your horoscope? Millions of people in the United States don't leave home without it—without reading it, that is. Are they "horoscope junkies?"

A daily horoscope for a Sun sign may read: "A good day for fishing. And we don't just mean for fish! Pay attention to possible catches, but throw back the little stuff." A horoscope junkie who pays attention to this forecast will pay attention to anything that they "catch" that day, from fish to advice—and probably for good reason.

What about the rest of us, who read our horoscopes "sometimes" or "never"? Are we heading for possible ruination, or worse? Of course not. But it might not hurt us to check our horoscopes a little more often. After all, you listen to the weather report before you go outside, don't you? C'mon, we know you do.

Sample Daily Horoscopes

Capricorn (December 22 to January 21)	Down to-earth goats may do better close to home today. Be precise and get those details right (or make sure your partner does!).
Aquarius (January 21 to February 19)	You'll enjoy having company today. Someone who knows *exactly* what he or she wants may benefit from some extra understanding. Is this you?
Pisces (February 19 to March 21)	Put your dreaming on hold long enough to get chores done—you know the ones we mean! In the evening, well, hang a sign: Gone fishin'!

Free Will versus Destiny—What's It All About?

As you may have already come to suspect, astrology connects your outer world to your inner world in order to reveal your potentials. And free will is there, too, available to you—if you seek to really understand yourself and become conscious of your unconscious behavior.

Your horoscope can reveal the lessons that you need to learn in your life. You may need to realize, for example, when you let others pull your strings and why, and then seek to reclaim that part of yourself. Or, if your soul has come to have a certain type of experience or learn a particular lesson, there's nothing that's going to prevent it (except, maybe…death), even if your conscious self is completely unaware of it.

Fate and free will are actually two very different things. It's possible to predict, for example, that you're going to have major changes to your home life in a certain time period, based on your present cycles.

Now you could take the bull by the horns, so to speak, and decide you're going to make that move you've been wanting to make for a long time during that period, or you could remodel or make some other changes to your home. Or, you could wait to get evicted, or for the house to get hit by a tree or by lightning!

In the first example, you have choices and you make them: this is free will. In the second, if you choose to wait for an eviction or catastrophe, it could be called fate.

To put it another way, whatever you need to learn, you are going to learn—whether your conscious self wants to or not. This also could be called fate.

So in the areas where you have lessons to learn, you really don't have a choice, except whether you're going to cooperate and make it easy on yourself—or not cooperate and make it hard on yourself. In other words, you do have choices—free will—but they're not about whether you can avoid learning your lessons; that's called fate.

Can You Believe Your Daily Horoscope?

The daily forecasts in the newspapers are Sun sign horoscopes only. Your Sun sign may be a dominant feature of your chart, but it's certainly not the only one. The Sun, in fact, is just one out of at least 40 different elements shown in your chart. Yes, a Sun sign reading applies to everyone with that Sun sign, in the same way that every person needs to eat a balanced diet. But each person's individual diet needs are different because of the infinite ways you can mix and match these 40 elements.

Sun sign forecasts are very general. You can be undergoing severe stress and difficulties because your own personal cycles are at a very challenging point, even though your Sun sign forecast is all cheery and nice for that day. On that same day, however, someone may say something nice to you. Now, it's not going to be enough to overcome the larger crisis—but it can make a difference.

So, can you believe everything you read in the papers? If your Sun sign forecast is written by a reputable astrologer, absolutely. These forecasts are rather general, but astrologers are looking at more than just your Sun sign to make them—they're looking at the planets and their cycles, and the relationship of the planets to your Sun sign. All of this added together can color a day in a certain way.

Of course, we can't answer the larger question about believing everything you read in the papers: You might want to take some of the things other than your daily forecast with a grain of salt.

And What About Those Hot Lines?

Ah, hot lines. These are the toll phone numbers you can dial to get your astrological reading for the day. What can we say? Well, for starters, the rates for these hot lines can be very high, usually well over what you would pay a certified astrologer for a session—as much as 200 percent over that amount, in fact. Many hot lines charge $3 per minute, and that's an hourly rate of $180.

Written in the Skies

Certified astrologers have not only studied astrology, but also have taken professional tests to become certified. These tests are tough. The testing sessions usually last at least eight hours, and sometimes go for days.

Now there aren't many astrologers who charge that much—and if they do, it's often because they're highly experienced and highly skilled, with tremendous knowledge. Hot lines, on the other hand, are often staffed with people who may know some astrology, but usually not enough to be actual astrologers.

Many of these so-called "astrologers" are purported to be working out of their homes—the phone calls are passed through to them when a caller comes through. There may not be anything wrong with this setup, but it's also not clear what kind of equipment and skills they're using.

Whether the hot-line person is actually doing the client's chart while they're on the phone with the client, for example, is unknown. Some of these people may not even have the software and computer to do the charts, and instead may simply look up the client's birth date information in a book, and then answer questions based on that. It may be better than nothing, but this sort of treatment would certainly provide incomplete information.

Out of Orbit

Before you decide to spend your money on a hot line, check with your local certified astrologers first (you can find them in your local phone book). You could save yourself a whole lot of money—and end up with far better advice.

If, on the other hand, you went to an actual astrologer, not only would you pay far less and get more accurate and better information, the astrologer would prepare and study your chart and current cycles before meeting with you, in order to get oriented to your needs, challenges, and path.

Because every chart is quite different, there is literally a mystery in every chart just waiting to be unlocked and revealed. No telephone hot-line person is going to be prepared enough, either in training or adequate analysis time, to evaluate and unlock these important aspects for you.

To be fair, though, hot lines are convenient and don't require appointments. But it can be expensive—and may yield wrong, or inadequate, information.

So we say *caveat emptor*. That's Latin for "let the buyer beware."

Going Beyond the Stars

Once you realize the connection between you and the rest of the world, you also realize that astrology is everywhere. First of all, it's about you—and about everyone else. It's about your relationships, and health, and jobs, and money—and it's about why you (and everyone else) behave the way you do. In addition, astrology is about your evolutionary purpose and what your soul came to learn and experience.

Astrology is also about the sky; in fact, some astrologers call the study of birth chart astrology "the inner sky." When you stand outside at night, beneath a sky filled with stars, planets, comets, and meteorites (and satellites and airplanes and maybe a UFO or two), you're reliving the human-sky connection where astrology began.

Astrology connects you with everything. Remember Sunday School, where you learned that "God is in everything"? Remember those physicists, discussing the inner order and the outer order? Both of those concepts are about the same thing—that astrology goes beyond the stars, to the place of each individual in the universe, and the place of the universe in each individual.

We don't yet know for certain what's "out there" beyond the stars, but just the fact that our imaginations take us there again and again should be enough evidence that we are connected with whatever may be there. *Star Trek, Star Wars, Star Man,* or *Stargate*—perhaps we intuitively know more than we realize.

When Sigmund Freud first unveiled his theories of the unconscious, they were called revolutionary—by everyone except astrologers, that is. Astrologers had been studying the effects of the hidden self on the visible self for thousands of years; they just didn't call it the unconscious.

Just as therapy may reveal your childhood, your dreams, and your hidden hostilities, astrology can reveal things about yourself you may not be aware of. By looking at your birth chart, you could discover that you have a tendency toward secretiveness and why, or what your chart reveals about your power struggles with your father and other authority figures.

Astrologically speaking, your unconscious is not really hidden. Rather, you might say, it is "written." All you have to do is "read" what's there.

Chapter 3

Your Horoscope and You

A Map of the Heavens Just for You

It looks like a wheel, or a pie, or yet another odd distribution of your taxes by Uncle Sam. But no—it's your astrological chart, a metaphor for you, designed for the day and the time and place that you were born. To take it a step further, an astrological chart (also called a birth chart or a horoscope) is a map of the heavens for the location,

date, and time you were born, and its symbols represent
the locations of the planets on that map. The sample
chart is for film director Steven Spielberg. Each of the 12
sections of the circle is called a house, and the mysterious
symbols represent the signs and the planets. Soon, this
chapter will unlock the mysteries of these symbols for
you. Later, Chapter 4 will return to Steven Spielberg's
chart and unlock some of his secrets as well.

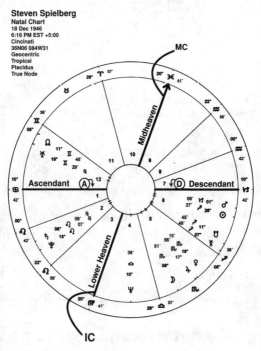

Steven Spielberg's birth chart.

You'll note a heavy, horizontal line through the center of
Spielberg's chart. This is called the horizon, and the sign
that was rising in the east over the horizon at your time of
birth is called your *ascendant*. Everything above it was in
the visible portion of the sky at the moment you were

born, while everything below it wasn't visible. The left end of this line is the east, not the west, as it is on maps. It helps to visualize this if you imagine yourself standing on top of the world, facing south, at the moment of your birth: east is on your left, right?

Star Words

Your *ascendant* is your rising sign, the sign that has just risen over the horizon at the moment of your birth. It represents the "you" that the outside world sees, as well as your personality traits, needs, and physical characteristics.

A Closer Look at Those Mysterious Symbols

Now take a look at Spielberg's birth chart. First, notice the information in the top left-hand corner: It shows Spielberg's birth date, birth time, and birthplace: 18 December 1946, 6:16 EST, Cincinnati, OH, and Spielberg's chart is calculated for this date, time, and location. Had he been born at another time, place, or date, the chart would be different from what's shown here.

The symbols in Spielberg's chart represent the location of the planets, and the signs they were in, at the time, date, and place of his birth. Think of the center of the chart as the position of the earth—and the placement of the planets as what's in the sky all around it. Now, the highest point of this chart (the upper, heavy vertical line on Spielberg's chart, marked with an "MC") represents the highest point that the Sun reached on the day of his birth. Note, too, the horizon line; this is the heavy horizontal line across Spielberg's chart. Its left is the east horizon, and its right is where the Sun sets in the west. Your ascendant, or rising sign—the mask you wear for the world—is the sign at the easternmost end of this line (marked with an "A" on Spielberg's chart).

The lowest point in the chart (the lower, heavy vertical line marked with an "IC") would be the exact opposite side of the earth from the MC, or the midheaven. The midheaven is the highest point that the Sun reached on the day of your birth. Your IC, or lower heaven, is the point on your birth chart that represents your life's foundations and psychological roots. It's found on the exact opposite side of the earth from the midheaven. Your *descendant* represents how you relate to others through partnerships and relationships. It's the sign next to the horizon (center line) on the right side of the chart and is marked with a "D" on Spielberg's chart.

Star Words

Your *descendant* is the cusp of your seventh house, and represents how you channel your energies through partnerships and relationships. Your midheaven, or MC, represents your ambition, career, or social role and public image.

The following tables show you which signs and planets are represented by which symbols. Each planet represents your different energies, and parts of yourself. Each sign manifests those energies in different ways, and all these things combine to make you who you are.

The Signs and Their Symbols

Astrological Sign	Symbol
Aries	♈
Taurus	♉
Gemini	♊
Cancer	♋
Leo	♌
Virgo	♍
Libra	♎
Scorpio	♏
Sagittarius	♐
Capricorn	♑
Aquarius	♒
Pisces	♓

The Planets and Their Symbols

Planet	Symbol
Sun	☉
Moon	☽
Mercury	☿
Venus	♀
Mars	♂
Jupiter	♃
Saturn	♄
Uranus	♅
Neptune	♆
Pluto	♇
North Node	☊
South Node	☋

Soon, you'll learn that there's more to your chart than what you see here. For now, all you need to remember is that your chart shows the position of the heavens at your birth—just as Spielberg's shows his universe.

Energies, Qualities, and Elements—Oh My!

Each of the twelve Sun signs is categorized in a number of ways. First of all, there are two energies, or genders, and each sign is either one or the other. Then there are three quadruplicities, called qualities, each of which appears in four signs. Lastly, there are four triplicities, each of which appears in three signs; these are called elements. Let's take all that a little more slowly. People born in signs with the same energy, quality, or element will have certain things in common. For example, people born in signs with a cardinal (or first) quality are likely to be leaders; and people with Sun signs that have an air element may always seem to be thinking or communicating.

Written in the Skies

Each combination of energy, quality, and element appears in only one sign. Aries, for example, has a yang energy, a cardinal quality, and the element of fire. Once you understand what each of these characteristics represents, you also can begin to understand certain aspects of an Aries personality.

➤ A Sun sign represents the position of the Sun in the heavens at the moment of your birth. When someone asks you what your sign is, he or she is referring to your Sun sign.

➤ The energies represent whether the energy manifested by a Sun sign is yang—direct and externally oriented, or yin—indirect and internally oriented.

➤ Qualities represent different types of activities and are related to where in a season a sign falls. Cardinal signs begin each season, so they like to begin things; fixed signs, in the middle of each season, are preservers, keeping things as they are; and mutable signs occur as the season is changing, and so are associated with transitions.

➤ The four elements describe the basic nature of the signs and of life: fire, earth, air, and water, each representing very distinct temperamental characteristics.

Energies: Are You a Flower or a Bee?

Every sign is either direct or indirect, male or female. You'll see the energies called "feminine" and "masculine" in some books, but we prefer to call them yang (direct/masculine) and yin (indirect/feminine), which avoids all that gender-based nonsense. All fire and air signs are yang, while all earth and water signs are yin. Each energy has certain characteristics that, coupled with the qualities and elements, create a unique picture for each sign.

The Signs and Their Energies

Yang	Yin
Aries ♈	Taurus ♉
Gemini ♊	Cancer ♋
Leo ♌	Virgo ♍
Libra ♎	Scorpio ♏
Sagittarius ♐	Capricorn ♑
Aquarius ♒	Pisces ♓

Yang signs tend toward direct action rather than waiting for things to come to them, like the bee that pollinates the flower. Yang represents the outgoing, the positive electrical charge, an external orientation, and the direct, "male" side of things. Yin represents the indirect forces and actions, those that understand what is needed to attract and create the desired outcome, like the flower that blooms in order to attract the bee. Yin is also called the receptive, the negative electrical charge, an internal orientation, and the "female" side of things. Yin/Yang. Black/white. Positive/negative. Up/down. Internal/external. Two halves of the same whole. That's all there is to it.

Out of Orbit

Avoid getting caught up in the old male/female dichotomy here. If you're a male in a yin sign, or a female in a yang sign, it doesn't mean you need to research hormone therapy. It simply means your sign has an energy that is one-half of the natural life force of everything that lives.

Qualities: The Way You Do the Things You Do

The qualities represent different types of activity. Think of the way a season progresses, from its forceful beginning, its fixed middle, and its transitional ending. This is what the qualities represent: each season, as it moves through its paces—and its three signs. Because each of the three qualities points to four signs, they're called the quadruplicities. Signs that share a quality share certain characteristics as well.

The Signs and Their Qualities

Cardinal	Fixed	Mutable
Aries ♈	Taurus ♉	Gemini ♊
Cancer ♋	Leo ♌	Virgo ♍
Libra ♎	Scorpio ♏	Sagittarius ♐
Capricorn ♑	Aquarius ♒	Pisces ♓

➤ **Cardinal.** The first quality, for the first sign in each season (Aries in spring, Cancer in summer, Libra in autumn, and Capricorn in winter), is called cardinal. People with cardinal quality signs are independent; they seek to move ahead, to start new things, and they can be proactive and enterprising. They also can be impatient if others don't move as quickly as they do, but they're independent, too—the signs of beginnings. In addition, once they get something started and established, cardinal people tend to lose interest in the project—instead, they're off to start something else. Remember, it's a certain type of person who likes to start things, and if you've got heavy cardinal influences in your chart, you're just that kind of person.

➤ **Fixed.** In the midst of each season, we have what is called the fixed quality. People with fixed quality signs (Taurus in spring, Leo in summer, Scorpio in autumn, and Aquarius in winter) are consistent, reliable, determined, and persistent. They often have great reserves of power, but they also can become stubborn, or set in their ways—these are, after all, characteristics needed to preserve what has already been started. Remember, though, that people with fixed quality signs are the ones who, once cardinal people have started things, take over from there.

➤ **Mutable.** The end of each season signifies a time of change, and so the signs in this placement are called mutable. People with mutable quality signs (Gemini in spring, Virgo in summer, Sagittarius in autumn, and Pisces in winter) adapt easily, are flexible and resourceful, are quick to learn, and can see issues from more than one angle. They also can lack perseverance, but this is precisely because they're adaptable and flexible. That's what's needed to make transitions—after all, they've already seen the beginning and the middle of the process.

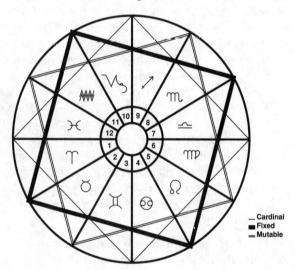

___ Cardinal
■ Fixed
___ Mutable

The Quadruplicities: The qualities form a square.

Elements: Your Natural Tendencies

Think of the elements as tendencies of the temperament: fire, earth, air, water. Everything that exists is comprised of these characteristics, and every astrological sign manifests one of them as well. In addition, all fire and air signs are yang, and all earth and water signs are yin. Because there are three signs for each element, they're called the triplicities. And signs that share an element share certain characteristics, depending on what that element is.

The Signs and Their Elements

Fire	Earth	Air	Water
Aries ♈	Taurus ♉	Gemini ♊	Cancer ♋
Leo ♌	Virgo ♍	Libra ♎	Scorpio ♏
Sagittarius ♐	Capricorn ♑	Aquarius ♒	Pisces ♓

➤ **Fire.** The first element is fire. Fire signs (Aries, Leo, and Sagittarius) are energetic, idealistic, self-assertive, courageous, and often visionary. If you remember that fire is first, it may help you to remember that fire signs are very active, stimulating creative expression, and always passionate. People with lots of fire planets are often known as "fireballs."

➤ **Earth.** The second element is earth. Earth signs (Taurus, Virgo, and Capricorn) are practical and skillful, good at managing physical assets, financial matters—or any form of matter. Think of earth signs as down to earth and you also will remember their characteristics. People with lots of earth planets are sometimes called "dirtballs or mudheads."

➤ **Air.** The third element is air. Air signs (Gemini, Libra, and Aquarius) represent social and intellectual abilities, ideas, communications, thinking, and social interrelationships. People with air signs operate on a mental plane, through air, so to speak, which may help you to remember what air signs are like. People with lots of air planets are often known as "airheads" or just plain "spacey."

➤ **Water.** The fourth element is water. Water signs
(Cancer, Scorpio, and Pisces) are sensitive and emotional; they think with their feelings, intuitively,
and are often romantic. Cancer represents the lake,
Scorpio represents the river, and Pisces represents
the ocean. If you think of water as emotion, you will
remember the characteristics of water signs. People
with lots of water planets are often known as "water
babies" or "cry babies."

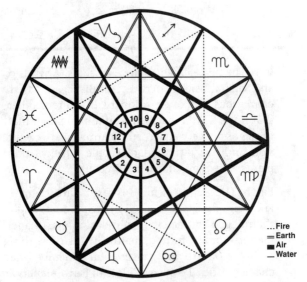

The Triplicities: The elements form a triangle.

Now that you know a little bit of the basics of reading
your birth chart, it's time to look at your Sun sign, the
strongest representation of who you are.

Chapter 4

You've Got the Sun in the Morning and the Moon at Night

In This Chapter

➤ Your Sun sign is the strongest representation of you

➤ Where was the Sun in the sky when you were born?

➤ Planet power: Where do you put your energy?

➤ Each house is an area of your life

The Sun Shines Just for You

Just as the Sun is the strongest light in our solar system, your Sun sign is the strongest representation of who you are. It's not the only one, but it's what you'll notice the most, because it's like the fuel you burn. Symbolically, the

Sun represents your self, your willpower, and your creativity. And mythologically, the Sun represents the Source, the unlimited resources of God.

Remember that the Sun's symbol ☉ is a perfect circle, an endless whole—and many believe that God, people, and people's creativity are interconnected. Man, so the story goes, was made in God's image, right?

When you look at Steven Spielberg's chart in Chapter 3, you'll see that his birth date is December 18, 1946. This means that Spielberg's Sun is in Sagittarius. Now we already know that Sagittarius has a yang energy, a mutable quality, and fire as its element. Just for fun, let's try translating this into the beginning of a chart reading for Spielberg.

People with yang energy signs tend to take charge of things, right? And Sagittarius, with fire and yang, is energetic and visionary as well. Add in Sagittarius's mutable quality, and you find people who are not only comfortable with change, but welcome it.

Steven Spielberg is a director—a person who takes charge. And a person who makes at least one film per year must have boundless energy as well.

But it's in Spielberg's films that you really begin to see his chart revealed. There's that "visionary" aspect, for example. Spielberg's list of film credits includes *Close Encounters of the Third Kind, E.T.,* and, on a very different note, *Schindler's List,* a movie that took an enormous amount of courage to make.

All of these films show a singular and forward-looking vision, a vision that also is shown in this very small glimpse of Spielberg's chart. Add to that a person who welcomes change, and you begin to see that Spielberg's chart is more than just a metaphor for him.

So What Exactly Is a Sun Sign?

Most people know their Sun sign, but not everybody knows just what that means. As we've explained, your Sun sign is probably the strongest representation of who you are. But who decided just where the Sun signs begin and end, and why they are the way they are?

Out of Orbit

We'd better warn you that Sun sign dates vary a little bit from year to year, so if you were born at the beginning or end of a sign, you may need to have your horoscope calculated to determine which Sun sign you have.

Remember those ancient astronomers, watching the apparent movement of the sky over Earth? Well, they're back! Part of their sky-mapping determined that the Sun went through certain constellations at certain times of the year—and that people born at that time of year seemed to share certain characteristics.

Now this isn't really so mysterious: there's some scientific evidence to suggest that people born at night may be night-owls, for example, and that people born in the summer may love warm weather. But if you know anything about astronomy, you also know that the constellations are not overhead at the times of year the zodiac indicates. So what's going on here?

A very long time ago, the constellations of the signs were in the area of the sky that was named for them. But due to the earth's wobble, and the fact that the earth shifts a tiny bit in space over a long period of time, the constellations have shifted out of those positions. So Western astrology uses the seasons, which don't change over time, as its basis for Sun signs, and has kept the names the same.

Find your Sun sign on the Zodiac wheel.

You Are Astronomically Unique

No one has the same birth chart as you: the odds of that happening are astronomically small. We've seen those odds calculated as high as 10^{312} to one against two people having the same chart, a number that would take up this whole book if you chose to write it down.

Now this number reveals something of the complexity of astrology—and the complexity of people—something no other model about people is able to do, except maybe DNA. No other models can come up with so many different combinations. Translation: You are unique!

Remember, now, Sun signs are just the beginning of astrology. Every one of the signs appears somewhere on your birth chart, and every sign is a part of who you are in some way. It's time now to look in more detail at planets and houses, because there's a whole lot more to you than just your Sun sign.

The Moon, and the Other Planets

As your self, your willpower, and your creativity, your Sun is the strongest representation of who you really are. For simplicity, the Sun and the Moon are called planets, too, because from Earth's vantage point they move across the sky just as the *planets* do.

Star Words

The *planets* are the celestial bodies that move through the zodiac in regular, predictable ways. In astrology, this includes the Sun and the Moon and the other eight planets: Mercury, Venus, Mars, Jupiter, Saturn, Uranus, Neptune, and Pluto.

Planets represent different energies within ourselves and our society. They're divided into:

➤ Personal planets (Sun, Moon, Mercury, Venus, and Mars)

➤ Social planets (Jupiter and Saturn)

➤ Transpersonal planets (Uranus, Neptune, and Pluto)

In addition, every planet has a symbolic representation, which is used as a sort of abbreviation when it's placed on a birth chart. The following table introduces each planet's symbol, and the energies of each planet.

The Planets

Planet	Symbol	Energies
The Personal Planets		
Sun	☉	Self, essence, life spirit, creativity, willpower
Moon	☽	Emotions, instincts, unconscious, past memories
Mercury	☿	Mental activities, communication, intelligence
Venus	♀	Love, art, beauty, social graces, harmony, money, resources, possessions
Mars	♂	Physical energy, boldness, warrior ways, action, desires, anger, courage, ego
The Social Planets		
Jupiter	♃	Luck, abundance, wisdom, higher education, philosophy or beliefs, exploration, growth
Saturn	♄	Responsibilities, self-discipline, perseverance, limitations, structure
The Transpersonal Planets		
Uranus	♅	Sudden or unexpected change, originality, liberation, radicalness, intuition, authenticity
Neptune	♆	Idealism, subconscious, spirituality, intuition, clairvoyance
Pluto	♇	Power, regeneration, destruction, rebirth, transformation

If Planets Could Talk...

Planets are the "what" of astrology. As you've read, they represent the various energies of a person, including things like mental and emotional nature, desires, vitality, soul, will, consciousness, and subconscious, as well as the people in a person's life.

Every planet, in other words, tells a story. And many of these stories you already know. Remember Icarus, the silly boy who flew so close to the Sun that his wax wings melted? Remember wrathful Neptune, god of the sea?

We think that each planet's stories are connected to the way that planet seems to behave, and so, in turn, they are stories about you. These stories are based on a number of things, such as what sign a planet is in and where it is in your chart, as well as which planets it associates with— and how well they get along with each other.

Astrology is complex, just like the planets, but in this book we don't have room to tell you the planets' stories. We hope you're interested enough to check them out in *The Complete Idiot's Guide to Astrology*. That book describes each of the planets in each of the signs and houses, and along with that information, we tell you their tales.

Who's in Charge?: Planetary Rulers

Every planet "naturally rules" one or more of the signs, and so, also naturally, certain planets and certain signs share certain characteristics. *Planetary rulership* means that a planet is "in charge" of a sign. For instance, no matter what sign Mars or the Sun is in, they are still in charge of Aries and Leo, respectively. And Leo, like the Sun, is bright and optimistic, while Aries, like Mars, is energetic and on-the-move.

Star Words

Planetary rulers are in charge of certain signs, and so these planets and signs share certain characteristics

Following are the planets and the signs they rule:

Planetary Rulers

Planet	Sign(s) Ruled
Sun ☉	Leo ♌
Moon ☽	Cancer ♋
Mercury ☿	Gemini ♊, Virgo ♍
Venus ♀	Taurus ♉, Libra ♎
Mars ♂	Aries ♈, coruler of Scorpio ♏
Jupiter ♃	Sagittarius ♐, coruler of Pisces ♓
Saturn ♄	Capricorn ♑, coruler of Aquarius ♒
Uranus ♅	Aquarius ♒
Neptune ♆	Pisces ♓
Pluto ♇	Scorpio ♏, coruler of Aries ♈

Planet Power: The "What" of Astrology

Which signs your planets are in can help you to see why you behave the way you do. If your Mercury is in Gemini, for example, it may indicate that you're a person who's quick-thinking.

Some people have several planets aside from their Sun in the same sign—but in a sign other than their Sun sign. This means they'll exhibit strong characteristics of that different sign. Similarly, some people may have lots of planets in a particular area of their chart, and so they may spend a lot of energy in that area of their lives.

Just remember that whatever signs your planets are in describe how you use their particular energies or functions in your life. For example, a Leo Moon means you will seem emotionally sunny and optimistic, while with an Aquarian Moon, you may seem emotionally aloof and detached.

Houses: The "Where" of Astrology

Now, looking at the graphic below, it's time to discuss what those pie slices really represent: they're the houses, the places where everything in your life occurs. Each of the 12 houses encompasses a specific arena of life, the stage where the drama of the planets unfolds. Everything in your life happens in one of these houses—from where you brush your teeth to where you keep your secrets. When you look at a chart, the first house is always the pie-slice just below the eastern horizon, and the other houses follow, counterclockwise, around the chart.

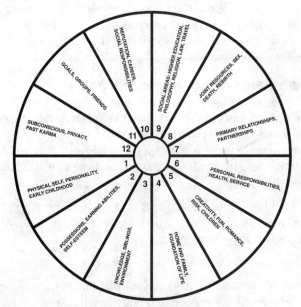

Where everything happens: The 12 houses.

Written in the Skies

Are you starting to wonder how you're going to keep this all straight? It may help if you remember that planets are the "what," signs are the "how," and houses are the "where."

It may help you to think of the houses as representing the horizon at the time of your birth: half the sky was visible, and half of it was not. Below the horizon are the six houses of personal development—invisible, but oh-so-important. This includes areas such as your personality, personal resources, knowledge, home, creativity, health, and responsibilities.

Above the horizon are the six houses of your development in the larger world—those that are visible, in other words. These houses include areas such as your relationships, joint or shared resources, social concerns, career, goals, and the subconscious.

Each Area of Your Life Has a House

Bear in mind that the chart shown above is just the tip of the iceberg when it comes to what's in each house. We've tried to give you word associations that you'll be able to remember. Planets in signs appear in houses, or, in other words, show how you do what you do in certain areas of your life.

Which house and sign a planet is in is where the story of you really begins. This is where the particular mathematics of astrology come into play:

Planets + Signs + Houses = *You*

If you've got Mars in Aries in your first house, for example, you're always going to put yourself first!

There's nothing arbitrary about these divisions: astrologers have been studying what's going on in each house for thousands of years—and these correlations are borne out again and again in the way we all behave.

Is There a Planet in the House?

In addition to being connected to each other through rulerships, signs and planets also are associated with certain houses. What we're going to show here are which planets and signs are naturally associated with each house. Remember, though, where your planets are depends on your chart.

In addition, don't forget that if you have more than one planet in a particular house, that's going to indicate an emphasis in that area of your life, and just what that emphasis is depends on which planets are in which house. Whew!

Also, just as certain planets naturally rule certain signs, they also rule certain houses. And which planet rules which house is determined by which planet naturally rules the sign on the *cusp* of the house.

Star Words

Cusps are the beginning of each house. The ascendant, for example, is the beginning of the First House, the house of self, and the next cusp is the beginning of the Second House, etc. The cusps also separate the houses from each other.

Now, in Steven Spielberg's chart, the Seventh House appears to be "empty." But look at that house's cusp sign: it's Capricorn, which is ruled by Saturn. Now the Seventh

House's natural ruling sign is Libra, and its natural ruling planet is Venus, so the Seventh House is the area where your primary relationships happen.

For Spielberg, with no planets emphasized here, it may initially seem to you that this would not be a major arena of his life. But notice that Saturn, the ruler of his seventh house, is in his second house near Pluto, a very powerful planet. This indicates that Spielberg has very important and powerful relationships, and that these people are also part of his personal resources.

The following figure shows you which signs and which rulers and corulers appear naturally in each house. These associations relate directly to what we just mentioned in Spielberg's chart—and they'll have an impact on your chart as well.

Natural planets and natural signs in their houses.

Chapter 5

Ascendants: A "You" for the World

1ˢᵀ HOUSE SWEET HOUSE

In This Chapter

➤ Ascendants, or rising signs, are the "you" the world sees

➤ The lessons you'll learn

➤ What is your ascendant? How to find out

➤ All about *your* ascendant

Your ascendant, or *rising sign,* is the sign that was rising over the horizon at the moment of your birth. This sign is your outward manifestation—the "you" that the outside world perceives. At the same time, though, your ascendant also is the way you express yourself (which is probably why the outside world perceives you that way).

Usually, your Sun sign and ascendant are different, which is why your ascendant is perceived as a "mask"—most of the time, hiding your true self, your Sun sign.

Each of the 12 signs rises over the horizon during a 24-hour period, so in rough terms, each ascendant rises over the horizon for two hours (more or less, depending on how quickly a particular sign rises) every day. In addition, whichever sign the Sun is in will be the sign rising at sunrise that day.

Star Words

Your ascendant is your *rising sign*, the sign that was rising over the horizon at the moment of your birth. Your rising sign represents the "you" that the outside world perceives, as well as personality traits and needs, and your physical characteristics.

In the early spring, for example, Aries is rising at sunrise, while at sunrise in the middle of summer, Leo is rising. This means that if you were born at sunrise, both your Sun and ascendant would be in the same sign—and so others would see you behaving like your Sun sign. Or, to put it another way, rather than wearing a different mask, you'd behave like your Sun sign.

We'd like to add another dimension to your consideration of your ascendant, too: think of it as "training" for the person you are becoming. In other words, your rising sign indicates the skills and traits you're learning to develop during your lifetime. If you're born with a Scorpio ascendant, for example, much of what you do may be connected with learning about control, both self-control and a need to control others.

Your ascendant also may be revealed in the clothes you wear, your hairstyle, or any of the other ways you "show" yourself to the world. Your ascendant is as much a part of you as your Sun sign—but it's often more obvious to others.

Your Mask for the World

Remember how carefully you'd select who you wanted to "be" for Halloween? Your parents may have laughed at your insistence that you "had to" be Batman, or Snow White, or Luke Skywalker, or Hopalong Cassidy (we're probably dating ourselves here…).

Your ascendant is the daily costume you selected at the moment you were born: it's the mask you wear every day, the "you" everybody else sees. And it may be connected to whom you wanted to be for Halloween, too.

Finding Your Rising Sign

So how do you find your ascendant? The most idiot-proof way is to have a computer with the appropriate software find it for you, but there are some simplified methods that you can use—right this minute. All you need to know is the time and date of your birth. This method isn't fool-proof (or should we say, "idiot-proof"?), but it works much of the time.

As an example, let's find Steven Spielberg's rising sign.

1. The birth date and time are entered in the appropriate "slice" for the date and time of day Steven Spielberg was born.

2. Now, we'll draw the symbol for Spielberg's Sun sign in the same "slice" in which we wrote his birth date and time.

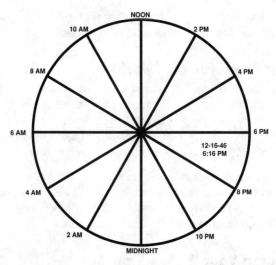

Steven Spielberg's birth date and time appear in the appropriate "slice" of the chart.

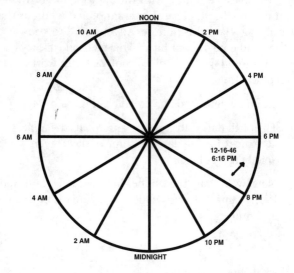

Spielberg's Sun sign symbol (Sagittarius) is drawn into the appropriate slice with his birth date and time.

3. Now, going in a *counterclockwise* direction, we've drawn in the symbols for the rest of the signs, in order, in each "slice." As Spielberg's Sun sign is Sagittarius, we follow with Capricorn, Aquarius, Pisces, Aries, etc.

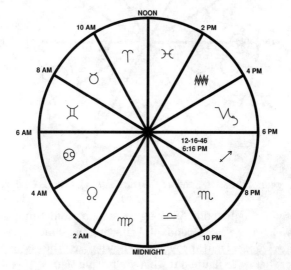

The signs are drawn counterclockwise on the ascendant chart.

4. Now, we look to see which sign is shown at the "eastern horizon" of Spielberg's ascendant chart. Remember, on an astrological chart, the "east" is on the left. "X" marks the spot. Note that the symbol for Cancer, in the house just below the eastern horizon, is circled. This sign is Steven Spielberg's ascendant.

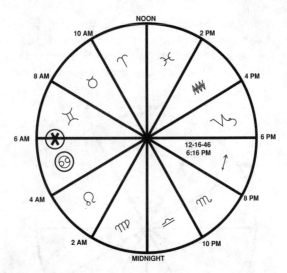

"X" marks the spot. Spielberg's rising sign, Cancer, is circled.

Okay. Enough about Spielberg. Let's figure something *really* exciting: your ascendant! Following the same procedures we just went through step-by-step, use the blank pie chart below to figure out what your rising sign is.

1. Write your birth date and time in the appropriate slice.

2. Draw the symbol for your Sun sign in the appropriate slice.

3. Draw the symbols for the other Sun signs *counterclockwise* on the chart in zodiac order.

4. "X" marks the spot.

To make things easier for you, feel free to refer to the zodiac chart below for the order of Sun signs and how to draw the symbols.

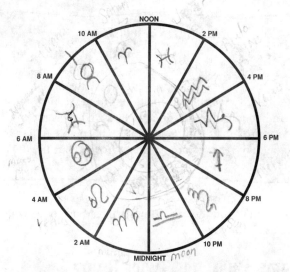

Use this blank chart with ascendant times to figure out what your rising sign is.

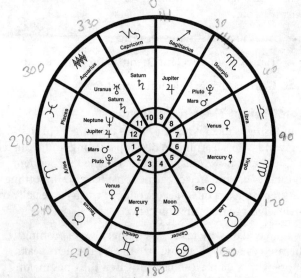

The zodiac symbols and the order of the Sun signs.

Written in the Skies

When you read the information for the ascendant you found using our pie chart method, if it seems all "wrong," read the information for the ascendants immediately before and after it as well. This method is approximate, not exact, and so it's possible that you may get a "wrong" reading from it: but it will be close.

Once you've found your rising sign, read on to see what it reveals about you.

Rams, Bulls, and Twins Rising

If you have Aries, Taurus, or Gemini as your rising sign, here's your "specialty" training, and the way others perceive you.

➤ Aries Rising: Striving forward

➤ Taurus Rising: Seeking identity through substance

➤ Gemini Rising: Emotion in motion

Ram Rising: The Aries Ascendant

Ram Rising is like taking the "Aries training." This is someone who's learning to develop a strong, individuated self, learning how to play, and to become independent, spontaneous, and free of restrictions. It's also important for them to learn qualities of courage, trust—especially in themselves!—and even innocence.

Ram ascendants are really ascending; always pushing themselves forward, always striving for the next peak. Those with a Ram ascendant are often the ones making the decisions, and they've got strong likes and dislikes to back up those decisions. But Ram ascendants may mistake impulsiveness for action and may not stop long enough to see what they really want.

Rising Rams may appear pushy or rude, but remember, an ascendant is a mask, and what appears to be arrogance may be covering up something else entirely.

Out of Orbit

You shouldn't think of your ascendant as an "excuse"; just because you've got Aries Rising, for example, doesn't give you a reason to run over everyone in your path. Your ascendant represents a "specialty" training you're here to take, and the sooner you master it, the easier life will be for you.

Bull Rising: The Taurus Ascendant

Rising Bulls seem placid and easygoing, have charming manners, and never impose their opinions on others. They don't want to upset the apple cart: they like it the way it is, full of apples!

You could think of Bull Rising as a "training" to learn about beauty: Rising Bull's lesson is to understand the nature of physical experience, aesthetics, and the nature of intimacy. As shamanic astrologer Daniel Giamarro says, the enlightened path for one with this training "is the Garden of Eden, to bring spirit into matter all the way, so one can totally enjoy it." This training helps Bulls learn to be fully present in life and increase their life force energy.

Bull ascendants seek their identity through substance, whether it be possessions, connections, or creation. Rising Bulls always seek to "keep a handle" on things, but their love of food, drink, and yes, sex, can make them momentarily forget that stability is their main pull. Like those with a Taurean Sun sign, Rising Bulls need to remember to love things for their own sake rather than for what they may represent. For Rising Bulls, possessions are merely a mask.

Twins Rising: The Gemini Ascendant

Motion. That's what you're going to see in a Rising Twin. Restlessness is the hallmark of this ascendant, and Rising Twins find their identity by making as many contacts as possible. Rising Twins are often the life of the party and, in fact, are often giving the party.

At the same time, Rising Twins are learning to be the eternal youth, free spirit, entertainer, artist, or comedian. They can also be the troubadour minstrel, the court jester, the trickster, the clown, or the coyote that leaves a surprise. Remember that the court jester was the only one who could tell the King the truth and not be killed for it (another form of messenger). Rising Twins are learning these abilities, as well as how to communicate truthfully without getting creamed for it.

A Gemini ascendant will appear excitable and quick—and also prone to upset. At the same time, there's an aloofness here: Twins' connections are made on a mental field, which can often leave the emotional out in the cold.

Rising Twins' motion may mask many things, but remember, an ascendant is just that—a mask. And if anyone knows how to wear a mask, it's a Rising Twin.

Crabs, Lions, and Virgins Rising

If you have Cancer, Leo, or Virgo rising, here's your "specialty training," and the way others perceive you.

➤ Cancer Rising: Learning responsible love and nurturing

➤ Leo Rising: Developing self-confidence

➤ Virgo Rising: A process of self-improvement and refinement

Crabs Rising: The Cancer Ascendant

Rising Crabs are talkative, especially about feelings, but also are moody and changeable, because their ruler, the Moon, changes signs every few days. Rising Crabs also are compassionate and receptive. They know what's happening with everyone around them, because they're sensitive to others. Family and traditions are important to them. But they can be crabby and irritable at times, too.

Rising Crabs are learning about the nature of family, home, and roots, as well as how to love and nurture so that their children will have a safe foundation and a concern for the welfare of generations to come. They also are learning how to responsibly nurture, love, and support their offspring or creative projects until they reach maturity—this is a "training" that teaches them how to redefine "family," while providing support and nurturing in an appropriate way.

Written in the Skies

It can seem deceptively easy to get to know a Rising Crab: they seem so soft and personal. But like those with Crab Sun signs, Rising Crabs wear a hard tough shell that may sometimes get in the way.

Rising Crabs may be indirect in their approach to things and may be quick to take things personally. Above all, they seem to react to all things emotionally—feeling rather than thinking. In the case of Crab Rising, there are two shells: the ascendant mask and the Crab shell itself!

Lion Rising: The Leo Ascendant

Rising Lions present the world with a bright, sunny, confident exterior, and a flair for the dramatic. How much has this got to do with the inner being beneath the show? That depends on you. One of the primary lessons of being a Rising Lion is to learn to give up needing other people's approval, respect, and admiration.

This usually doesn't happen until the person is able to choose self-approval and self-respect over that of other people. When it does happen though, Rising Lions suddenly gain more respect and admiration from others than they had when they were trying to please others. Self-approval is the key to a Lion Rising.

An ascendant Lion may help to develop self-confidence, because the outer person will be projecting self-confidence as a matter of course. After a while, this can become second nature, helping those less confident to actually overcome a lack of faith in themselves.

No other sign can mask quite so well as Leo, and no other mask can fit so well that you forget it's a mask. But beneath all the roar may be a real pussycat!

Virgin Rising: The Virgo Ascendant

When you meet Rising Virgins, the first thing you notice may be that they're refined and soft-spoken. A man with Virgin Rising may look like a quintessential British gentleman. They may not say much until they've adequately sized you and the situation up. Because these people are analytical, they'll probably ask you several questions, rather than assume anything. Rising Virgins also can be very witty people, because they're Mercury-ruled.

Rising Virgins often find one area of their lives to act as a place of purity, a way to keep some part of themselves apart from the contamination of everyday life. They seek their identities through a constant process of self-improvement and refinement, and while they give an appearance of ruthless efficiency, they are often masking something else entirely.

Rising Virgins are learning to develop a new understanding of how they can contribute to our present culture and the nature of sacred work in today's world. Once they understand what their sacred work is, they can learn to co-create with the patterns of the Universe.

Rising Virgins may be learning to put things in perspective, or they may have a tendency to let small details take on meanings far beyond their actual importance. Work will matter a great deal to Rising Virgos and may well be their most effective mask.

Scales, Scorps, and Archers Rising

If you have Libra, Scorpio or Sagittarius as your rising sign, here's your "specialty" training, and the way others perceive you.

➤ Libra Rising: Creating conscious, equal relationships and partnerships

➤ Scorpio Rising: The life force as a path to God, the Universe, or the Source

➤ Sagittarius Rising: Seeking adventure, new horizons, and spiritual growth

Scales Rising: The Libra Ascendant

Rising Scales often have refined and delicate features, a certain beauty and charm, and a manner of dressing that is always clean, neat, and in good taste—with a strong sense of style and color. They also may have a well-developed sense of diplomacy and refined social graces. Rising Scales are very personable and charming as well.

Rising Libras are learning about conscious, equal relationships, and partnerships. This is not about defining who you are by who you're with, though, but actually learning—through constant interaction—about relationships as a spiritual path. In addition, this "training" is about refining one's awareness.

Rising Scales' need for companionship or partnership is balanced by their desire for fair play, peace, balance, and harmony, and once their need for love is satisfied, their desire for social justice will kick in.

Scorp Rising: The Scorpio Ascendant

There's nothing halfway about a Rising Scorp; they put the whole force of their personality behind everything they do. Rising Scorps are often very magnetic and attract others very easily: their magnetism is one of the reasons it's so easy for these people to gain power—others give it to them. Another aspect of their personalities is their intensity. Someone once described this personality as similar to a holocaust survivor at a cocktail party! They aren't really interested in discussing the weather or other chit-chat, and their intensity may scare others.

Rising Scorps are learning about the life force as a path to God, the Universe, or the Source. As part of this "training," Rising Scorps may experience powerful and intense feelings, which they will then learn to master in order to fully understand their experiences.

Scorp Rising is a strong indicator that these people are born with a need to control, because that's when things feel safest to them. There may have been major difficulties in the early environment and home life that encouraged them to take control so they would feel safe—and remember that people don't worry about feeling safe unless they feel very vulnerable. Rising Scorps' greatest challenge is to learn how to control themselves, and to stop controlling others.

The mask of Scorpio is secrecy; Scorpio Rising can act as a double disguise. Rising Scorps may use manipulation or deception to rise to power, and they may move quietly in the wings until their rise has been completed.

Written in the Skies

Many of the 20th century's most influential leaders have had Rising Scorps: Gandhi, Mussolini, Lenin, and Stalin. So while it's clear that Rising Scorps' quest for power is separate from questions of good and evil, it's equally clear that it's a given.

Archer Rising: The Sagittarius Ascendant

The world of Rising Archers is filled with possibilities, and these people are unusually optimistic. Rising Archers are explorers—they need to see new territory—so goals and challenges are very important to them.

Rising Archers often have long thin faces, with high foreheads, rather like horses, in fact, and they may shake their heads, just as horses tossing their manes. Rising Archers tend to hide their problems and troubles behind humor, and they don't want others to be worried about them. Part of this is because they can't stand to worry about themselves, so they don't want others to do so either.

With their strong philosophical outlook and/or strong religious nature, Rising Archers believe that something better is just around the corner, even when things go wrong. And Rising Archers always seem to be shooting their arrows in order to have new challenges and goals—having to do the same things over and over again drives them crazy.

With Jupiter as the ruler of their ascendant, Rising Archers are often jovial, happy-go-lucky, enthusiastic, and optimistic, seeking always to find the truth, and they will approach the world as if it's their own oyster, filled with possibilities. Rising Archers are like trainees on a Star Fleet spaceship, learning "to boldly go where no one has gone before." They are learning about the meaning of life and expanding their inner selves to the furthest horizons possible. Adventure and spiritual growth go hand-in-hand with Archer Rising.

Goats, W-Bs, and Fishes Rising

If you have Capricorn, Aquarius, or Pisces as your rising sign, here's your "specialty" training, and the way others perceive you.

➤ Capricorn Rising: Being responsible for yourself and for others

➤ Aquarius Rising: Progressive forward-thinkers

➤ Pisces Rising: Learning how to give in a healthy way

Goat Rising: The Capricorn Ascendant

Rising Goats are learning about what it means to be responsible for not just themselves, but others, too. Part of this "training" is learning the rules, and part is being available to help others, but the tough side is that Rising Goats may begin to believe that they are responsible for all the problems around them (rather like a scapegoat!) and that they must carry the burden for others.

Rising Goats would better help themselves by learning how to oversee their territory, as well as learning new ways to create family and community.

Rising Goats may be worriers: they'll worry about what's going wrong in their youth, what can go wrong in their middle age, and about death in their old age. And they can tend to be quiet and reserved, though this often masks an active mind and tremendous willpower.

It's often hard for Rising Goats to show their feelings; their mask of reserve may be doubly thick because Capricorn is a naturally quiet sign. What you'll find on the surface with a Rising Goat is a need for order, a constant checking of the details to make sure everything is going smoothly—and a sometimes obsessive certainty that it's not. It's all part of learning about responsibility.

Rising Goats may remind other less-practical signs that they need to attend to what matters, and so they sometimes seem to be "wet blankets." But underneath all this careful planning, you may find someone who's a whole lot of fun.

Water-Bearer Rising: The Aquarius Ascendant

Rising Water-Bearers (W-Bs) appear to be forward-thinking and progressive, friendly, and open to new ideas, but they also may be intolerant of others' shortcomings and quite sarcastic.

In fact, Rising W-Bs are full of contradictions: they love to travel, and they love to stay at home; they're friendly and outgoing, and they're moody and aloof. Mind-wise, they can be both scientific and artistic, and they may be involved in two very separate areas of work.

Rising W-Bs are magnetic—and associated with electricity—so people with this rising sign appear unusual in some way and attract many people to them. This is often the ascendant of celebrities or people who work in broadcasting. Rising W-Bs are taking the "training" of achieving cosmic consciousness. They're here to learn how to detach from the physical and emotional planes so they can focus on spirit and the higher planes.

Always, though, W-B Rising goes forth with a spirit of adventure. They may forsake human connections for ideas,
but no matter what, they are always on the cutting edge.
Take Carl Jung, for example; he had an Aquarius rising!

Fishes Rising: The Pisces Ascendant

Rising Fishes want the world to appear ideal, and if it
doesn't, they'll ignore anything that doesn't color the picture the way they want. Rising Fishes sometimes show
endless goodwill toward others, often to the detriment of
themselves, and will often get caught up in pipe dreams
and get-rich-quick schemes, both their own and others.

Rising Fishes need to learn about giving in a healthy way,
including giving unconditional love to everyone—not just
family, clan, tribe, or race—as other signs do. This "training" teaches them to be there for others and to merge
themselves and their energy with others, in order to help
anyone that needs it.

Rising Fishes also are learning how to be in the flow of
life, instead of trying to control things. This is a "giver
training," but Rising Fishes also learn to offer help to anyone—not just those who look, think, and act like them.

Quick to be sentimental, Rising Fishes will cry over
anyone's spilled milk. Their bodies are basically one big
antenna, catching all the pain and pleasure the world has
to offer, and their moods will change as often as the
tides—or even more often. Rising Fishes' eyes may be
watery looking, and have an ethereal look to them.

The mask here is feeling, a curious mask, because feeling
would seem to be an internal sense. But the Rising Fishes'
seemingly quick emotions may be covering something
else entirely—or they could just be the tip of the iceberg.

Chapter 6

In the Beginning: Aries, Taurus, and Gemini Sun Signs

In This Chapter

➤ Aries, Taurus, and Gemini are the first zodiac signs

➤ Aries ♈, the Ram: But(t), I'm *first!*

➤ Taurus ♉, the Bull: Down to earth, and plan to stay there

➤ Gemini ♊, the Twins: Thinking out loud

The first three zodiac signs, Aries, Taurus, and Gemini have little in common: Aries likes to get things going; Taurus likes to keep them as they are; and Gemini likes to talk about them! They do have one thing in common, though: they're all signs of spring.

Aries, the Ram: But(t), I'm FIRST!

First Zodiac Sign

Aries, The Ram ♈	March 21st–April 20th
Element:	Fire
Quality:	Cardinal
Energy:	*Yang*
Rulers:	Mars and Pluto
Color:	Red
Gem:	Diamond
Anatomy:	Head and face
Keywords:	Pioneering, leading, new beginnings
Mythological Archetypes:	Luke Skywalker, the Virgin Amazon, the Marlboro Man
Celeb Rams:	Marlon Brando, Eddie Murphy, Diana Ross, Gloria Steinem, Tennessee Williams

Star Words

This is the symbol for Aries, the Ram. ♈

The Ramifications of Being a Ram

➤ How many Aries does it take to screw in a light bulb?

➤ One, but you better get the hell out of the way.

It's no accident that Aries is the first sign; if it hadn't been, it would have rearranged the zodiac to get there! Aries is the sign of the pioneer, of the daredevil, of the person who just won't say "no." In legend, the Ram often came to the rescue, and, in fact, that's how Aries ended up as a constellation—as a reward from Jupiter for trying to save some children from the machinations of their wicked stepmother.

Nothing can stop the Ram; as the first of the cardinal signs, no one has a stronger will. Rams want to be where the action is and will do anything to make sure they get there first. Don't stand in a Ram's way—you're likely to get run down by this Butthead of the zodiac!

Rams are the only fire sign with a cardinal quality, which means they like to start things, but may not want to finish them. Because they're also a fire sign, they're enthusiastic and impulsively go off to start something without giving it much thought beforehand. Fools rush in where angels fear to tread, true, but rushing in takes great courage, and Rams have plenty of that!

Written in the Skies

Qualities represent different types of activities and are related to where in a season a sign falls. Cardinal signs—Aries, Cancer, Capricorn, and Cancer—start each season and are signs of beginnings.

The symbol for Aries, ♈, could be interpreted to represent the eyebrows and the nose—the face, in other words, the part of the body that's under Ram's rulership. Or it could be interpreted as a sign of the emergence of self, of beginnings. It also represents the constellation Aries, which can be found in the sky standing erect, its head facing toward Mars.

The Best and Worst of Ram

Rams are assertive, direct, and straightforward, but this also means that they can be aggressive, blunt, or impatient. Strong-willed Rams can be remarkably single-minded once they have a goal in sight, but this single-mindedness can make them tactless, blind to side issues, or just plain irritating.

Rams like challenges and are often wonderful leaders. Their courage can inspire others to follow their lead, and their confidence and enthusiasm get everybody where they're going.

But anyone who likes a challenge also likes a good fight, and Rams can be argumentative. At their worst, they're steamrollers, running over anything that stands in their way. But at their best, Rams are idea people who can inspire others to help those ideas see the light of day.

Rams in Love

Rams in love won't take "no" for an answer; they'll pursue their beloved to the ends of the world—and beyond, if necessary. Rams have the happiest love matches with other fire signs: other Aries, or Leos, or Sagittarians; signs who, like Ram, crave excitement and passion.

In fact, if those fires don't keep burning, don't expect Rams to stick around. They like relationships that can contain the fire, and may seek lovers who are dependent on them for love but independent in other ways.

Rams can be jealous; they expect their love to give them the same fiery attention that they're giving. But Rams also enjoy sharing everything with a lover they trust, and their ambition for those they love, like their ambition for themselves, knows no bounds.

Rams and all air signs do well together: Ram's opposite, Libra, for example, can provide some air to keep the fire burning, but Ram may get tired of Libra's standards. The other air signs, Gemini and Aquarius, can also feed Ram's fire. But Ram is not a "householder" sign and that's one reason why it doesn't do well with Cancer and Capricorn. Love requires compromise and meeting the needs of others, and this is very hard for Rams to do!

From a mythic point of view, Aries is the Marlboro Man, the Rugged Individualist, the Virgin Amazon, Wild Woman, or even the goddess Diana or Artemis. None of these types are high on settling down to build a nest, especially when they're young. These are adventurers, and they don't care much about dirty dishes or sniveling kids.

The Healthy Ram

Aries rules the head and face and also represents the eyes and the brain. With this influence, it's easy to see why Rams are the quick thinkers of the zodiac, and therefore prone to injuries because they sometimes leap before they look. At the same time, because they're quick to anger at both real and imagined slights, Rams may be susceptible to headaches and nervousness. The best health advice Rams could get would be to slow down—but don't expect them to listen!

Written in the Skies

One of the most important lessons Rams can learn is cooperation. If they learn that the help of others can only further their own creativity and desires, they can move beyond their Ram-centeredness and make enormous marks on the world.

Mars, Aries' ruler, represents the blood and iron, and so Rams need to get enough iron to keep them oxygenated, to keep their hemoglobin up. They also need vitamin B12, which is required for the formation of red blood cells and metabolism, and potassium, which is necessary for maintaining their muscles and heart rate.

Rams at Home

There's never a dull moment with a Ram at home. Like adolescents, Rams see all the world has to offer—and want to experience it all, too. But, also like adolescents, Rams may see that world from a self-centered point-of-view, and that can make life with a Ram a challenge. One thing's for sure—don't expect to find Rams snoozing next to the fire. They're the ones throwing more logs on, just to see what happens!

Rams at Work

Rams need work that holds their interest, things that totally involve them and allow them the freedom to express themselves. They don't like to take orders, and they'll always try to climb to the top themselves. Their love of competition means that they won't let setbacks stand in their way, and their eagerness for new experience means they'll jump whenever they see a new opportunity.

Rams are often found in positions that need "idea people"; they're project leaders—as long as there's someone else around to handle the details. Rams also do well in creative fields, where their fiery independence can find self-expression.

Some Aries like to work outdoors—like the archetypal Marlboro Man, for example, or in construction, which is even more common—and many prefer work that enables them to maintain their independence. This can include things like outside sales, consulting, or contract work.

Rams and Their Money

Impulsive Rams sometimes spend first and think later—or don't even bother to think later! Money for a Ram is one more way of getting ahead, and getting ahead is Ram's credo. Rams can be—and often are—generous, especially when it comes to pursuing something or someone they want. With money, though, Rams might do well to turn their cash over to an earth sign; someone who won't burn it quite so quickly. They'll often be the ones to see ways to make money, but it may just as often be others who take advantage of Ram's moneymaking ideas.

Taurus, the Bull: Down to Earth, and Plan to Stay There

The Second Zodiac Sign

Taurus, The Bull ♉	April 20th–May 21st
Element:	Earth
Quality:	Fixed
Energy:	*Yin*
Ruler:	Venus
Color:	Green
Gem:	Emerald
Anatomy:	Neck and throat
Keywords:	Ownership, dependability, sensuality
Mythological Archetypes:	Aphrodite, Osiris
Celeb Bulls:	Candice Bergen, Henry Fonda, Jack Nicholson, Michelle Pfeiffer, Harry Truman, Queen Elizabeth II

Star Words
This is the symbol for Taurus, the
Bull.

♉

The Bull on the Bull

➤ How many Tauruses does it take to screw in a light bulb?

➤ One, but she'll do it when she's good and ready.

No one is more down to earth than the passive, fixed, earth sign, Taurus. All of Bull's feet are planted firmly on the ground, and Bull's calm and dependability make a Bull a friend you can count on. Hand in hand with that dependability, Bulls can be conservative and cautious, so they're usually perfectly happy with the way things are.

At the same time, their connection with the earth means they're often materially wealthy, but Bulls' wealth can also be found in the cozy homes they create: Bulls like to sit calmly in their favorite chair, maybe smoking their favorite pipe or reading their favorite paper, perfectly content if nothing ever changes.

But this desire for harmony goes beyond the self: Bulls also seek a harmony with everything on earth. You're likely to find Bulls living in the country, but even if they live in the city, you'll find them surrounded by plants or working in their garden. Bulls crave silence, too, the silence that comes with inner serenity, and they are often people of few words. Bulls are the most physical of the signs—everything they know, they know through the body. This is because they're ruled by Venus, the ruler of the senses.

In ancient Egypt, Osiris, the God of the Dead and the Underworld, was represented as a man with a bull's head.

Living manifestations of Osiris were selected by the priests and revered. Osiris remains with us today—look on the back of a one-dollar bill: there's an eye (the symbol of Osiris) above a pyramid!

Aphrodite also represented Taurus—after all, Taurus is ruled by Venus—and she represented the qualities of deep intimacy, as well as beauty. She was beautiful not to attract men, but to celebrate herself and her high standards. She was intimate only with those men who met her high standards for honor and love!

The Best and Worst of Bull

At their best, Bulls create a calm in the midst of storms all around them. They're connected solidly to their bodies and to their homes, have good jobs, good friends, good marriages, and good children. They're the people everyone else turns to: they're who you call if you have a flat tire at 2 a.m., and, though they may be reluctant to get out of bed, they'll be the ones you know you can rely on.

But in their complacency, Bulls may be resistant to change, and can become dogmatic or even preachy. Bulls can't understand what all the excitement's about, and they may be the first to tell you all this New Age stuff is a lot of bunk. Bulls can be lazy as well—too comfortable to get out of that chair, or they can get so caught up in their earthly possessions that life itself passes them by.

Bulls in Love

Security and stability—a Bull in love stays in love. Romance and love are one and the same to sensuous, earthbound Bulls, and they're nothing if not patient when it comes to making sure that the love they find is the right one. A Bull will always be there for you—and expects the same in return.

Bulls don't like change, so they may show some jealousy if the stability they create seems threatened in some way.

A Taurean partner is one you can always depend on, though, and, although it may seem dull at times, you can rest assured they're with you for the long haul.

Bulls are attracted to water signs, especially Cancer and Pisces. But many Bulls or Rising Bulls find their mate in a Scorpio, Bull's *opposite*. Bulls get along well with householder Cancer, as Bulls like their comfort. Remember—earth and water go well together, creating beautiful lakes.

Star Words

Opposite signs, or a polarity, are signs that appear directly across from each other in the zodiac. Taurus and Scorpio are opposites.

Taureans are often attracted to the more lively signs like Aries, Gemini, or Sagittarius, but quickly become annoyed when all these signs want to do is go out and play. They're most comfortable with other earth signs, whose reliability and need for established routine matches their own. Don't expect many fireworks here, though—just everything in its place as it should be!

The Healthy Bull

The Bull rules the neck and throat and so the entire metabolic system. The thyroid gland in particular can be a problem for Bulls: they may not properly convert what they eat into energy and so can be prone to gain weight. Their love of inaction feeds this tendency as well. But the throat is also where singing comes from, and many Bulls are well-known singers—Barbra Streisand, Bing Crosby, and Ella Fitzgerald, to name just a few.

Iodine is necessary for the development and functioning of the thyroid gland, which is ruled by Taurus. Other vitamins and minerals that are important to Taurus are selenium, bioflavenoids, and vitamin E, which work together to maintain beauty and promote normal body growth, fertility, and metabolic action. With Venus being Bulls' ruler, getting enough of these nutrients is even more important than usual!

Bulls at Home

Home is where Bulls thrive: they collect, they arrange, they make it into a womb where they—and those they love—can comfortably relax. Bulls may be collectors, too: with their Venus ruler, they have an appreciation for beauty. Their homes may be filled with music and books as well as paintings and sculpture.

Bulls crave comfort, security, and calm, and their homes reflect that desire. A Bull's home is always a good place to show up at dinnertime. Not only will there be something wonderful cooking, but you're sure to be invited to stay!

Bulls at Work

No one knows a good opportunity like a Bull, especially an opportunity that promises long-term stability. Even Merrill Lynch knows this: they're "bullish on America," remember? Connected to the earth, Bulls can do well with real estate or land deals. But Bulls don't want to build the homes and buildings so much—Aries does that—as they want to own the land, home, or building as an investment.

Their connection to the earth makes them practical in nature. They aren't going to set off on an impulsive whim. They may be interested in finance, for example, or banking, or the things they can build with money and resources.

Bulls make wonderful employees, too: they're the ones who show up even on snow days, the ones who get the proposal in on time. Because Venus is their ruler, many Bulls are talented folks who sing, write or perform music, sculpt, or enjoy other creative endeavors. Many Bulls use their voices for voiceovers or are radio announcers or disc jockeys.

Bulls and Their Money

Bulls are wonderful providers and may acquire a great deal of money and many possessions. But they also need to be careful not to cross the line into materialism, wealth for its own sake, or extravagance. Bulls can be greedy, too, hoarding their money or hiding it away where it will be "safe." But as the ultimate Taurean desire is for earthly harmony, they are far more likely to use their wealth to share their desire for comfort with those they love.

Out of Orbit

There's nothing wrong with a little security, but Bulls need to beware of taking it to extremes. If Bulls' love of possessions crosses the line from comfort to acquisition, they may lose sight of enjoying things in the here and now. Bulls need to beware of becoming so prepared that there's nothing to enjoy now.

Gemini, the Twins: Thinking Out Loud

The Third Zodiac Sign

Gemini, The Twins ♊	May 21st–June 22nd
Element:	Air

The Third Zodiac Sign

Quality:	Mutable
Energy:	*Yang*
Ruler:	Mercury
Color:	Yellow
Gem:	Agate
Anatomy:	Hands, arms, shoulders, lungs
Keywords:	Mentality, communication, versatility
Mythological Archetypes:	Castor and Pollux, Coyote, the Trickster
Celeb Twins:	George Bush, Clint Eastwood, Judy Garland, Bob Hope, Marilyn Monroe, Sally K. Ride

Star Words

This is the symbol for Gemini, the Twins.

♊

Twin Tales

➤ How many Geminis does it take to screw in a light bulb?

➤ Two.

Twins never miss a thing; their goal is to see everything. Gemini is a mutable sign, which signifies change; a yang sign, which signifies motion; and an air sign, which signifies the mind. In their quest for knowledge, Twins are always in motion, always alert, trying to live not just two, but as many lives as they can, all at one time. Often called a dualistic sign, Twins are really deceptively simple: it's all based on avid curiosity, on finding things out and then quickly moving on to something else.

Twins have been called the Great Communicators, too, and with Mercury as their ruler, it's easy to see why. But sometimes words can mask meaning, and that's another paradox of Twins: meaning is not really what they're after—it's the ideas themselves.

The symbol for Gemini, ♊, may be merely the Roman numeral II, but it also may represent the parts of the body ruled by this third sign: the hands, arms, shoulders, and lungs. Taking it still one step further, this symbol could represent the dual sides of human nature: mind and soul. On the other hand, maybe it is just a pair of twins!

The Best and Worst of Twins

Twins can be amusing, witty, quick, and flexible—and they can be glib, sarcastic, fickle, and devious. Two sides of the same coin, and all too easy for a Twin to flip back and forth between them. At their best, Twins are masters of invention, clever and adaptable, never afraid to try something new. But this same eagerness to try everything can lead them to be scatterbrained or restless, even unreliable or ungrateful.

At their weakest, Twins can run themselves to emotional exhaustion, or feel that nothing matters. At their strongest, their wide variety of interests brings them many friends and experiences, and their quick mind enables them to take it all in. You can always count on a Twin to be the life of the party!

Twins' flexibility and adaptability arise because this is a *mutable* sign—and mutability means changeability. They also are very resourceful because they've seen so much, and that's part of their mutability too—the more you're willing to change, after all, the more you're going to see.

Star Words

Mutable signs, such as Gemini, occur as the season is changing and so are associated with transitions. Other mutable signs are Virgo, Sagittarius, and Pisces.

Twins in Love

The Twins of the Gemini myth, Castor and Pollux, chose to be united forever in the sky rather than separated for even a moment—and so Gemini is obviously a sign of relationships. Translated to love, though, Twins have so many relationships that they can all seem a little too casual. This is because Gemini's a mutable sign, and it's not that a Twin won't give you all the attention you want, it's that a Twin can't—there's too much else going on!

Here's where Twins' fickleness can come into play: someone who seemed fascinating last week is a known quantity this week and so is no longer interesting. But Twins also can be the ideal partners: they're charming, witty, generous, and genuinely interested in you—it's keeping that interest that's the hard part. Meet them on their own ground—wit and imagination—and let them know they can trust you by trusting them.

Other air signs—other Geminis, Librans, and Aquarians—are always a good bet for Twins; air signs are lighthearted and understand each other's need for mental stimulation. At the same time, though, two air signs may never come down from the clouds—and if they do, they may find there's no place to land.

Because air feeds fire, Twins can do well with Aries, Leo, and Sagittarius. Down-to-earth Virgo is a good match, too: with the same quality and ruler as Gemini, Twins and Virgos can challenge each other, and learn a lot from each other as well!

Healthy Twins

No other sign can benefit quite so much from learning to breathe, learning to relax, and to take deep breaths and then let them out. Twins are always on the move, moving their arms like wings much of the time, and all this rushing around can mean they don't stop and smell the roses like they should. Gemini rules the hands, arms, shoulders, and lungs, and this grouping reflects yet another of Twins' dualities—the need to flit about and the need to breathe deeply and relax. If Twins don't learn to relax, all that flying around can lead to emotional exhaustion.

Out of Orbit

No sign is more prone to the dangers of running in circles. Twins are so fond of motion that they may not notice that their motion isn't leading them anywhere. Over stimulation can lead to jumpiness, insomnia, or, as already mentioned, emotional exhaustion. Twins need stoplights or they'll never stop!

Twins need strong amounts of vitamin B-complex every day in order for their nervous systems to function properly, to keep them thinking, and to keep their metabolisms going. This includes all the B vitamins, and when Twins are under stress they need more than the normal dosage, because they'll use it up quickly. In addition, sugar and alcohol chemically deplete the B vitamins in the body, so it's best for Twins not to binge on those!

Twins at Home

Twins at home—now, there's a phrase that's hard to interpret: Twins don't often stay put long enough to let them see where home is. But maybe that's exactly it: Twins are at home wherever they happen to be. Twins are seldom content to sit still and watch the world go by; they'd rather be on that world and going by with it!

Don't forget that Twins are great communicators, so if they are at home, you're likely to find them on the phone or gathering new information from reading or watching TV.

Twins at Work

Twins need mental challenges to keep them stimulated on the job, and it can't be the same challenge over and over again. Careers like advertising, writing, broadcasting, and public relations appeal to Twins because they're always presenting new challenges to Twins' inquiring minds. Don't rule out technical fields, though; the right opportunity might offer Twins just the mental somersaults they need.

Twins are often found in sales positions or in jobs where there is a lot of contact with other people. They can be "silver-tongued" with their wit and communication abilities, so they're excellent at persuading or influencing others. This literally translates to selling products or services, or selling ideas to others, whether as a manager or a writer.

Twins and Their Money

Twins like to spend their money on information, computers, travel, and cars—things that will feed their need for new ideas, communication, movement, and action. Twins don't worry much about spending, either, and are apt to max their credit cards and then sign up for another. It's not money that concerns Twins; it's information—and any way they can get it, they will, including buying it.

Chapter 7

Home, Pride, and Perfection: Cancer, Leo, and Virgo Sun Signs

In This Chapter

➤ Cancer's your emotional side, Leo's your pride, and Virgo's at your service

➤ Cancer ♋, the Crab: Home is where your shell is

➤ Leo ♌, the Lion: Pride of the forest

➤ Virgo ♍, the Virgin: Serving the World

The signs of summer, Cancer, Leo, and Virgo, may share a season, but each is otherwise unique. Emotional Cancer is a nurturer; bright, sunny Leo seeks the spotlight; and meticulous Virgo improves herself by helping others learn about sacred patterns.

Cancer, the Crab: Home is Where Your Shell Is

The Fourth Zodiac Sign

Cancer, the Crab ♋	June 22nd–July 23rd
Element:	Water
Quality:	Cardinal
Energy:	*Yin*
Ruler:	Moon
Color:	Silver
Gem:	Pearl
Anatomy:	Stomach and breasts
Keywords:	Feeling, sensitivity, nurturing
Mythological Archetypes:	The Turtle, The Crab, Ceres
Celeb Crabs:	Tom Cruise, Princess Diana, Harrison Ford, Ernest Hemingway, Linda Ronstadt, Meryl Streep

Star Words

This is the symbol for Cancer, the Crab. ♋

Crucial Crab-iness

➤ How many Cancers does it take to screw in a light bulb?

➤ One, but her therapist has to talk her into it.

Touchy, touchy, touchy: no one else feels like a Crab. And no one retreats like a Crab, either: quick to hurt, they're also quick to crawl into their shells. But remember, these shells are also their houses. Crabs are nurturers, too: the Mamas and the Papas of the zodiac.

Others look to Crabs for warmth and understanding, and Crabs always lend a sympathetic ear, lap, or shoulder. But these Moon-ruled Moon Children won't look to get the same from you. They may be the most sensitive sign of the zodiac, but they're also the least likely to let you know what they're feeling. Crabs hide their emotions behind what they believe is an impenetrable shell.

Out of Orbit

Wound Crabs and they'll never forget it; Crabs will carry grudges for life. Befriend Crabs and they'll never forget either; Crabs are famous for keeping in touch with old friends, old loves, and old times. And what a memory!

For Crabs, it's all about security; in fact, that's the major point of Cancer. Crabs are learning about emotional and physical security, as well as responsible nurturing. After the primal instincts of Ram, the building of Bull, and the thinking and mental development of Twins, there's the emotional foundation of Crabs, which can take many forms, like a house—or a shell.

The Best and Worst of Crabs

At their best, Crabs are dependable, loving, adaptable, and self-sacrificing, which means at their worst, they're cling-ing, over-sensitive, moody, and smothering. Want a money manager? Let a Crab handle it. Need an advance?

Better have those numbers ready! Late for dinner? Tell Crab your sob story. Didn't show up at all? Better move to another town!

Because one of us is a Crab, we know how easily Crabs are distracted, and how anything can set Crabs' imaginations running—in another direction. Crabs are always off on tangents. Picture a crab on the beach, always moving sideways rather than forward. They do get where they're going, often without the rest of us realizing they've done it. Sneaky? Yes, Crabs can be sneaky. Clever? Yes, they're that, too. Don't ever take a Crab for granted, that's for sure. They'll leave you standing in the sand, wondering which way they've gone!

Many of Cancer's myths involve turtles or tortoises. In ancient Egypt, the constellation was called Stars of the Water, and its symbol was two turtles. In Roman mythology, the Crab also assisted Jupiter's wife, Juno, in trying to slow down one of the many labors of Heracles (Hercules in Greek mythology). The unfortunate Crab got caught underfoot, though, so all Juno could do to reward it was place it in the heavens!

Crabs in Love

No one sends more confusing messages than a Crab; just when you think they might be interested, off they go into their shells! Crabs are so afraid of being hurt that they may never let you know they're interested, but on the other hand, if they decide they've got a chance with you, look out! Crabs can hang on very tightly.

Crabs who didn't feel coddled as children may seem cold and distant as adults. But in their indirect Crab way, they're really dying for attention. Crabs have a natural fear of revealing themselves—those soft insides are very vulnerable—so they're never going to approach you directly. You know those conversations that go, "What's the matter?" "Nothing"? Chances are they're with a Crab!

Written in the Skies

As a water sign, Crabs require trust in a relationship and are very cautious about giving their hearts away. The things they need most are love and security, and even if you and a Crab later part, the Crab will stay in touch and remember your birthday. Deep down, Crabs really do believe love makes the world go 'round!

Water signs—other Cancers, Scorpios, or Pisces—understand things the same way Crabs do, and Pisces in particular may inspire Crabs to use their intuition. But Crabs are good with earth signs—Taurus, Virgo, and their opposite, Capricorn—keeping them watered and fertile. Gemini can be fun, but may feel smothered, and Leo may love the attention, but not return it.

The Healthy Crab

Nurturing Crabs rule the stomach and the breasts, sources of food and nourishment. So naturally, sensitive Crabs are prone to stomach troubles and, with their love of creating comfort through food, can also be prone to overweight.

No sign is as sensitive to touch, and Crabs are always reaching out and touching. But they're sensitive to hot and cold, too: you'll see Crabs wearing socks in July, or, if it's very hot, scuttling into the shade or the water to cool off. Remember that Crabs' ruler is the Moon, and the Moon has no light source of its own. Crabs reflect everything around them, and their emotions swing with the tides.

Vitamin A and beta carotene are especially helpful for growth and maintenance of all mucous membranes, including the stomach and digestive tract, which is very important to a Crab. They also help build strong bones and teeth (ruled by Capricorn, the opposite sign). Crabs also may have allergies, which are often aggravated by dairy products, so if digestion becomes a problem, it's best to monitor what they eat in relation to how they feel.

Crabs at Home

Crabs' homes are their safe havens—even if they do carry their houses on their backs! It may be the pillows tossed about for comfort, or it could be those good smells coming from the kitchen, but you'll always feel like a Crab's home is a place you can relax and unwind.

Within that cozy home, though, there's a place that's Crab's alone. It may just be a corner on a couch, but in that corner will be Crab's favorite book or blanket, and maybe a picture or two. Chances are Crab's dog or cat will snuggle up there, too, whether or not Crab's there at the moment. But rest assured there will be a dog or cat, or maybe more than one. Crabs nurture any creature that comes their way.

According to Greek (and Roman) mythology, Demeter (Ceres), goddess of the Earth, was responsible for agriculture and growth. When Demeter found out that Pluto (or Hades back then) had stolen her daughter, Persephone, and taken her to the Underworld, Demeter grieved and forbid anything on Earth to grow. Zeus (Jupiter) had Hermes (Mercury) go to the Underworld to strike a deal with Pluto.

Because Persephone had eaten seven pomegranate seeds and had done a tour of the Underworld, however, Pluto insisted that she be returned to him each year for three months (our winter months). So, Demeter is associated with Cancer, the sign of motherhood and responsible nurturing.

Crabs at Work

While it may seem that Crabs can be too dreamy or unfocused to do well in business, it often happens that the opposite turns out to be true. Intuitive and sensitive to change, Crabs can often sense future trends and be on the cutting edge.

Crabs are often found in creative areas like writing, too, because writing involves the part of motherhood that requires gestation, creating something new and unknown, and then birthing it. In addition, Crabs' empathy for others, as well as their prodigious memories, come into play with the creative arts, helping them generate works that connect with everyone.

Alternative ways that mothering may come out at work can be birthing new products, projects, or companies, taking care of others by feeding them, or nurturing their emotional selves via teaching.

Crabs and Their Money

Tenacious Crabs hoard their money just like they do everything; in fact, no matter how much they accumulate, they may never feel entirely secure. Crabs don't differentiate between things and security, and because of their nature (hard on the outside, soft on the inside), they hold onto everything with a tenacious grip.

Sometimes this hoarding tendency can move into selfishness, not because Crabs don't want to help, but because they're so afraid of being hurt from the outside that they'll do anything they can to protect themselves—including keeping all their assets to themselves.

You won't often find Crabs broke—they're far too concerned with security. And, because they want this security for those they love as well, they'll make sure to create a safe haven for them, too.

Leo, the Lion: Pride of the Forest

Fifth Zodiac Sign

Leo, the Lion ♌	July 23rd–August 22nd
Element:	Fire
Quality:	Fixed
Energy:	*Yang*
Ruler:	Sun
Color:	Gold
Gem:	Ruby
Anatomy:	Back, spine, and heart
Keywords:	Willpower, creativity, expressing the heart
Mythological Archetypes:	Kings, The Lion King, Hercules
Celeb Lions:	Lucille Ball, President Bill Clinton, Robert DeNiro, Mick Jagger, Madonna, Napoleon, Jacqueline Kennedy Onassis

Star Words

This is the symbol for Leo, the Lion.

♌

The Lion's Roar

➤ How many Leos does it take to screw in a light bulb?

➤ One, and a hallelujah chorus while he does it.

Talk about self-confidence, Lions invented it! Ruled by the Sun, Lions bask in the spotlight. They're dramatic, they're bold, they're creative, and they're strong; no other sign can grab and hold the spotlight the way a Lion can.

Lions are great fun to be around, too: their exuberance is contagious, and when they get to the party, everyone knows it's really begun. Not only can Leos lead, they will lead: Lions expect to be at the head of the line—and of the pride.

Lions don't give up, as anyone who has watched a lion chase and catch its prey can attest to. The point of being Lions is to be at one with the creative principle, and to learn how their willpower affects what they create in their lives. Self-expression and creativity are everything to Lions—eventually they learn to follow more than just their own will, aligning themselves with the higher Self and the creative principles of the Universe.

Why do so many Leos go by one name? Because they can! With the Sun as their planet, Lions live in and for the spotlight, and with that kind of lighting, they can go by any name they choose. Jackie, Lucy, Mick, Madonna, and Napoleon are just a few Leos we recognize from singular names. Others include Fidel, Tipper, and Lawrence (of Arabia).

The Best and Worst of Lions

Because Leo is a fixed sign, Lions can be determined, stubborn, or even habit-bound, but confident Lions are born to lead, and they're proud, courageous, and self-assured to a fault. Lions can be generous, commanding, ambitious, and proud, and this means they can also be intolerant, demanding, self-righteous, and vain. Lions can lead others to tremendous victories, but they can be ruthless with their enemies, though their memories are short and they also are quick to forgive.

Written in the Skies

It takes creativity to generate excitement, but Lions are among the most creative signs of the zodiac. The Sun, after all, provides illumination, and it is through that light that Lions truly shine.

Because Lions are always leading, they are often surrounded by yes-men and sycophants. This, in turn, can lead to gullibility, because Lions are easily flattered and can forget that not all may love them. And, as much fun as they can be, they also can become overbearing or self-centered if things aren't going their way.

Because Leo is a fixed sign, Lions are exceptionally loyal, and so expect loyalty in return as well. They are very up-front about their needs and expectations, and this lack of guile can also be their undoing; Lions might do well to trust a little less, but they expect adulation, and others can't help but give it to them.

Lions in Love

Generous Lions expect generosity in return: they love being in love—and the drama being in love provides. Lions are loyal too, which can actually make it difficult to end a relationship with them.

Lions expect adoration, but they'll give it as well. Like kings, they'll graciously give their loyal subjects all they can. A fire sign, they'll usually do best with other fire signs—other Leos, Sagittarians, or Arians—but Lions also can be caught up in the intensity of Scorpios or the refinement of Libras.

Airy Geminis, and Aquarians (Lions' opposite), are also a good match; remember that opposites attract. Lions learn a lot in particular from the detached Aquarian, who can provide them with perspective and give them balance.

The Healthy Lion

No one is healthier than Lions; the ailments that touch the rest of us seem to pass them by. This strength is due in no small part to Leo's rulership of the back, spine, and heart: even the words suggest Lions' strength.

But Lions can be less strong emotionally. When they fail to get the adoration and respect they deserve, they can become physically ill. And Lions, like all cats, can be lazy too; the only evidence of life in them may be the continual twitching of their long tails.

Because Leo rules the spine and heart, these areas also can cause them trouble when things don't go well. They may make a trip to the chiropractor or a cardiologist to get them back on track, but it's also important for them to deal with the underlying emotions that set off the problems to begin with.

Lions need plenty of magnesium and calcium on a 1:1 ratio to protect their hearts (a muscle) and circulatory systems. And Lions need to pay more attention to their potassium and salt balance than other people, because that balance is very important for their hearts. Coenzyme Q10, an enzyme that strengthens the heart, may also provide them with additional energy when they get older.

Here's an example of the Lion's strength: The only way Hercules could slay the Lion of myth was in hand-to-paw combat, and even then, the Lion managed to bite off one of Hercules's fingers! So awed was he by his opponent's strength, Hercules used Lion's pelt for a breastplate and his jaw for a helmet, both of which helped him in his further labors.

Lions at Home

Lions call their homes their "castles," and they love to show off their castles almost as much as they love to show off themselves. Lions give great parties and won't hesitate to keep the food and wine coming.

Home is another place where Lions' generosity is evidenced: there's always a place for everyone to sleep, and friends are welcome to stay as long as they please.

If they're not entertaining, you may find Lions roaring when they're upset, but you may also hear them purring like kittens when everything is in order and they get the attention they need.

Lions at Work

No one leads like a Leo, and Lions will naturally gravitate toward careers that allow them to shine. They may be generals or presidents, but Lions may be teachers as well, firing up their students' enthusiasm with their own.

And Lions can often be found in the performing arts, shining with the brightness of the Sun. In the public eye, a Lion is charismatic and magnetic, but even in less visible fields, a Lion always shines.

Above all, Lions need an audience (what good is it to be king without subjects?) and often choose jobs where they can get one. These fields include sales, teaching, consulting, tour guiding, management, and, of course, performing.

Lions are kings, and kings are Lions. The Lion of Judah and Richard the Lionhearted are just two examples, but don't forget the Queen of Sheba, daughter of the Sun (ruler of Leo) who married Solomon: according to legend, all their children, the Ethiopians, were destined to be kings. There's just something regal about the noble Lions, and it's got a lot to do with the way they carry themselves: these people look and act like royalty, even when they're not. Some American Lions? Jacqueline Kennedy

Onassis, Norman Schwarzkopf, and Bill Clinton. So you may have even more career choices than you think!

Lions and Their Money

Image matters a lot to Lions, so if the checking account balance and Lions' needs are saying different things, it's the needs that are going to win out. Big night out with the gang? Count on Leo, broke or not, to pick up the tab.

Nothing's too good for a Lion, so they're not likely to notice what something costs. In fact, Lions seldom think to bargain; when they see something they want, they get it. Living the good life, according to Lions, has nothing to do with what things cost, and this makes them most generous—nearly royal in their magnanimity!

Virgo, the Virgin: Serving the World

The Sixth Zodiac Sign

Virgo, the Virgin ♍	August 22nd–September 22nd
Element:	Earth
Quality:	Mutable
Energy:	*Yin*
Ruler:	Mercury
Color:	Blue
Gem:	Sapphire
Anatomy:	Intestines and colon
Keywords:	Service, self-improvement, sacred patterns
Mythological Archetypes:	Chiron, Mary, Astraea
Celeb Virgins:	Sean Connery, Greta Garbo, Michael Jackson, Stephen King, Sophia Loren, Lily Tomlin

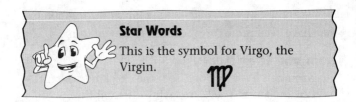

Star Words

This is the symbol for Virgo, the Virgin. ♍

Virgin Values

➤ How many Virgos does it take to screw in a light bulb?

➤ At least four. One to take out the light bulb, one to check the wiring, one to put the new light bulb in, and one to clean up the mess.

Purity. Perfection. Practicality. These are the Virgin values. But what does this translate to? Virgins, more than any other sign, are identified with analyzing, with examining everything in great detail in order to improve not just themselves, but the world. And improving the world means serving more than one's self: it means serving the greater good. Virgins are very responsible people.

But Virgins are about connection too: they see things very clearly, and they see each part of a whole in a way that few other signs can. One of us is a Virgo, and she is forever finding the little errors her coauthor didn't bother to reread for—and then, the next time through, she finds still more! This pleases her messy coauthor to no end, but it pleases Virgo as well: Virgins really like to clean these messes up! Constant refinement means no discord, and Virgo does whatever's necessary to achieve perfection.

There's a lot of misinformation about the use of the word "virgin." A virgin is a woman whole unto herself—not just someone who has never had sex. Virgins are about finding the patterns, especially sacred patterns, and in past eras, these were the people who were the sacred priests and priestesses. They also worked in agriculture, taking care to read the natural cycles and patterns correctly so there would be enough food to feed everyone.

In Native American tribes, Virgin is represented by the spider, which weaves the sacred patterns in its web. And Virgins aren't very comfortable in our present society because the sacred patterns have largely been lost or forgotten.

The Best and Worst of Virgins

Calm-on-the-outside Virgins will fool you like no other sign—on the inside they're all restless energy, constantly seeking, constantly improving, constantly fixing whatever needs to be fixed. Here is one of the zodiac's liveliest minds, a consummate problem-solver, a model of methodical efficiency, bent on beauty and perfection.

But okay, yes, Virgins can think too much. They can find fault wherever they look—even where there's none to be found. They can be inflexible, and they can worry too much along with all that thinking. But at the same time, because Virgins measure their self-esteem by weighing what they accomplish in a given day, they can increase their self-esteem by giving up this narrow view of what they're good for. Then they'll see themselves as whole people, with love, feelings, and other important things to offer others.

Because Virgo is an earth sign, Virgins are very practical, and because their quality is mutable, they're very resourceful. That same mutability also can translate into flexibility, and so Virgins can be chameleon-like, too.

Out of Orbit

Virgins may agree with you when they sense you're not going to change your mind (practical and flexible), but privately they won't change their minds either, unless it suits their purposes!

No one is more organized than a Virgin. While the rest of the world is collapsing around them, Virgins are calmly making lists of what's left. No one's more committed, either, or more willing to make sure it goes smoothly for everybody. If there's someone in the kitchen cleaning up after dinner while everyone else has gone on to another party, it's most likely a Virgin, who's probably perfectly happy to be there. Virgins like to work, and they do it very well.

Virgins have long been known as healers and those who serve, and the mythological archetypes here are no exception. Chiron was the wounded healer who couldn't heal himself but nonetheless healed others, and Astraea was a healer as well. And Mary, the Mother of Jesus, was chosen for that role because of her service to God and her purity.

Virgins in Love

There's no denying that Virgins are seeking the perfect mate, but they also enjoy the pleasures of intimacy, especially when those pleasures can lead to personal growth. In her constellation in the sky, Virgo appears to be dancing, and, in fact, one of her greatest joys is the fruit of consummated love.

Because Virgins like to serve, they will do whatever they can to take care of those they care about. Sometimes they can go too far, leaving the beloved with nothing to do, but often they anticipate the needs of others with prescient clarity.

As seekers of order, it's natural that Virgins seek out other earth signs—other Virgos, Taureans, and Capricorns—but it may be the fixed intensity of Scorpio or the mutable water of Pisces that really plants the seeds of contentment for this mutable sign. Watery Cancer, too, can make for strong emotional connections. But Virgins shouldn't necessarily settle for complacency just because it's tidy; they may find far more excitement with Gemini or Sagittarius!

The Healthy Virgin

Virgins are concerned with health and its application. Their ruler, Mercury, in an earth sign like Virgo, is very practical and interested in practical applications of knowledge. Virgins will often know about vitamins or about aromatherapy; they'll know which herbs cure which ills and why your antibiotic isn't working on your pesky cold. Virgins' interest in health is largely because they're interested in practical knowledge and in sacred patterns (and what's more sacred than healing?), as well as in keeping themselves healthy.

Virgo rules the intestines and colon, and it is in these areas that problems often arise for them. Busy Virgins need to stop what they're doing periodically to eat, and they need to relax while they eat, not rush through—or worse, work through—their meals. Virgins need to remember to serve themselves as well as they serve everyone else!

In addition, Virgins are most likely to get sick when they have problems at work (especially if they dislike going to work) largely because of their dedication to any given project. Workaholic Virgins need to balance work with relaxation and pleasure.

Virgins need a lot of B-complex vitamins to help control their anxiety. In addition, they need PABA (Para-aminobenzoic acid), which is important for maintaining the health of the intestines and breaking down and using proteins.

Virgins at Home

Here again, Virgins' love of service shows itself clearly. The Virgo home is tidy, efficient, and organized, but that just makes it easier to take care of all those who enter. You won't find Virgins sitting down to eat until everyone else has enough on their plates, and even then, Virgins may hover rather than sit down and join in.

Virgins are great lovers of beauty, and coupled with their understanding of botany, this can mean homes surrounded by lovely gardens and filled with thriving plants and herbs. Virgins are likely to have aloe vera growing over their sinks—and even more likely to snap off a leaf to rub on your wound!

It can be interesting, living with Virgins, and with all those "sacred" patterns they find with their family members.

Virgins at Work

Count yourself fortunate to have a Virgin on your work team—with their love of challenge and constant need for self-improvement, they'll bring a strong dose of clarity to any project.

Virgins can be good planners, good organizers, and good finishers, but the same knack for details can also make them very strong in any field where they use their hands. Best of all, no matter what they do, Virgins are always reliable, whether they're the boss or an employee. And with their desire to serve, they'll see the job gets done in a fine way.

The two largest job categories for Virgo are in the health field and any jobs that require analysis, including marketing, systems analysis, and computers. Virgins love details and excel at jobs that require them.

Virgins and Their Money

Detail-oriented, organized Virgins always have their checkbooks balanced and often know exactly how much money they've got in their pocket as well. Here's an area where Virgins, with their eye for every detail, can tend to be highly critical of their own abilities, but they are in reality not only able money managers, but also clever ones, staying within their budgets, never frivolous. In fact, you may often find that the folks we call "bean counters" are Virgins.

Chapter 8

Balance, Power, and the Search for Meaning: Libra, Scorpio, and Sagittarius Sun Signs

In This Chapter

➤ Libra, Scorpio, and Sagittarius are the signs of fall

➤ Libra ♎, the Scales: balancing both sides, now

➤ Scorpio ♏, the Scorpion: the power of one

➤ Sagittarius ♐, the Archer: seeking life's meanings

The signs of spring and summer represent personal development, and with the start of fall, we move into the signs of external development—Libra, the seeker of harmony; Scorpio, the transformer; and Sagittarius, the explorer.

Libra, the Scales: Balancing Both Sides, Now

The Seventh Zodiac Sign

Libra, the Scales ♎	September 22nd–October 23rd
Element:	Air
Quality:	Cardinal
Energy:	*Yang*
Ruler:	Venus
Color:	Blue
Gem:	Opal
Anatomy:	Kidneys, lower back, adrenal glands
Keywords:	Balance, harmony, justice
Mythological Archetypes:	Blindfolded Justice, Pallas Athene, Juno
Celeb Scales:	Presidents Jimmy Carter and Dwight Eisenhower, Jesse Jackson, John Lennon, Emily Post, Eleanor Roosevelt, Barbara Walters

Balancing Beauty and the Beast

➤ How many Libras does it take to screw in a light bulb?

➤ Maybe one to do it and one not to do it.

Star Words

This is the symbol for Libra, the Scales.

♎

Harmony. Balance. No one wants to even things out like a Libra. Libra begins at the autumnal equinox, a time when the length of the day equals the length of the night, and Scales strive for such balance in all they do.

Libra is the sign of justice and so is represented by a blind-folded Venus, who holds the scales of Libra in one hand and the sword of Mars/Aries (its opposite) in the other. The goal for Libra is the attainment of inner harmony and a reconciliation of opposites. Not an easy task, but if any-one can do it, Libra can!

Written in the Skies

The prime purpose of Scales is to create relationships with others. Libra is the opposite of Aries, where people are concerned with them-selves. Here we see the concern for others and the incorporation of both perspectives, "mine" and "theirs."

Libras are charming, and their charm is primarily due to the rulership of Venus. Scales see everything from both sides and have a great appreciation for art and beauty. As a yang, cardinal sign, they generate a great deal of activity as well, especially in starting things, like diplomatic rela-tions with others.

But Libra is an air sign as well and, like all air signs, has an active mind. In Scales' case, this takes the form of look-ing at one side and then the other, weighing everything over and over again. Like other cardinal signs, Libra seems constantly in motion, starting new things, and taking initiative.

The Best and Worst of Scales

Scales are social creatures, ready to share their experience with others, and quick to form partnerships. Friendly, popular, and attractive, they often are idealistic as well, eager to talk about their high principles and lofty ideas with any who will listen.

But Scales can seem affected or insincere, too eager to compromise, or worse, indecisive. Scales are often so busy weighing each side of an issue that they can never come to a conclusion or decision. Also, in their need to please others, they may forget to please themselves. Scales need to be aware of their own needs and meet them, too, not just those of other people.

Scales are at their strongest with other people, and yet their focus in a relationship is on themselves. Scales' self-concept is a reflective one, seen through others' eyes rather than their own. At the same time, though, Scales may hide their own feelings in order to give an appearance of balance. Scales would do well to remember that making a decision is not always a tipping of the scales!

At their best, though, Scales understand that their strength lies in creating and maintaining relationships. Scales seek to find their perfect complement, their other half, to complete the balance. They also want to find balance in other things, not just relationships.

Scales in Love

Scales love to be loved and admired, and they give much in return as well. Constantly testing their powers of attraction, they may seem flirtatious and flighty, but all the while Scales are seeking their other half. Scales are romantics, too, and they love to "set the mood" for romance by creating an atmosphere of beauty to match their feelings.

Air signs—Geminis, Aquarians, other Librans—with their easy talk and quick minds, are an obvious match for

Scales, but there are interesting possibilities with Scales' opposite, Aries, as well—though each sign may believe the other too selfish. Scales can thrive with Leo's generosity, or they may find the balance they seek through an adventure with Sagittarius.

Out of Orbit

Ruled by Venus, Libra's particular romanticism is often a search for an ideal mate, and Librans should beware of the disappointment that can occur when such high expectations are brought down to Earth. Scales also may refuse to acknowledge the beloved's true self and instead keep their partner up on a pedestal.

Healthy Scales

Graceful Scales should pay attention to inner fitness as well as outer fitness; their tendency toward lower back or kidney problems is a direct result of keeping things inside to avoid creating discord. As in love, healthy Scales need to bring their ideals down to an earthly scale!

Scales also can benefit from holistic aids like aromatherapy, and the lovely scents and properties of rose oil or jasmine can help create the inner harmony Scales seek. As a sign ruled by Venus, after all, Scales are very sensitive to smells all around them.

For Scales, extra potassium may be needed to balance the water level in the body and stimulate the kidneys to eliminate wastes. Vitamin E, selenium, and vitamin P (or bioflavonoids) are very helpful for preserving the beauty of Libra.

Scales at Home

Scales' homes are lovely places, filled with objets d'arts, reflections of the beauty of Librans themselves. True to their need for others, Scales are among the great hosts of the zodiac, filling their homes with other people as well as those people's conversations, ideas, and, often, their music.

Scales also enjoy the comforts of life and will not hesitate to make certain that their home reflects them. Because Scales seek harmony and balance above all, this is what you will find in their homes.

But all that waffling we've mentioned can make life with Scales rough going at times. Their constant weighing of things can make decision time difficult, and their ideals can mean they seek a harmony impossible to find here on Earth. Still, this reflects in a home that is singularly lovely, as befits the home of a Venus-ruled sign!

Scales at Work

Social Libras shine at work: they are often leaders, showing others the way, but with their need for balance and harmony, they are often partners, too, using their knack for balance and harmony with others to achieve great things.

Scales' charm comes into play at work, too: They often have a knack for public relations or sales. Or Scales' love of beauty may translate into a career in the arts, or in fashion or interior design.

You might expect Scales to be judges and lawyers, but though they often are found in these fields, their tendency to vacillate rather than come to a final decision can sometimes hamper them.

But these same qualities can make Scales fine counselors, where their ability to hear two sides of an issue rather than take sides is a decided asset. And for the same reason, they can be remarkable teachers, translating a broad array of ideas into a range of possibilities.

Scales and Their Money

Money for Scales is a means to an end, and that end is beauty and harmony. Scales need to be aware, though, that things and their appearance cannot give or replace inner security and harmony, and in fact, they may find that hanging on to a little "mad money" could bring them much closer to such balance than they would have thought possible.

Scales are more likely to invest in things and people than in long-term securities, because they like to see an immediate return on their investment—in the form of beauty and harmony. The inward reflects the outward here as in no other sign: to Scales, appearances really do matter.

Scorpio, the Scorpion: The Power of One

The Eighth Zodiac Sign

Scorpio, the Scorpio ♏	October 23rd–November 22nd
Element:	Water
Quality:	Fixed
Energy:	*Yin*
Rulers:	Pluto and Mars
Colors:	Burgundy, Black
Gem:	Topaz
Anatomy:	Genitals, urinary and reproductive tracts
Keywords:	Desire, transformation, power
Mythological Archetypes:	The Phoenix, Persephone, The Scorpion, Grandmother Spider
Celeb Scorps:	Bill Gates, Georgia O'Keeffe, Dan Rather, Winona Ryder, Hillary Clinton

According to Navajo myth, Grandmother Spider is the Grandmother of all the people (the Dineh, as the Navajo call themselves). Whenever the people seem lost or confused, it is Grandmother Spider who will speak to them from her ever-evolving web, to remind them that they already know the way—and that they must simply look inside themselves!

Star Words

This is the symbol for Scorpio, the Scorpion. ♏

Scorpio's symbol, ♏, is a pictorial representation of a scorpion's stinger connected to the human reproduction organs, and in ancient times it also represented the mythical phoenix, a bird that continually regenerated from its own ashes. Scorpio also is said to represent the serpent in Adam and Eve, and an eagle. One thing's clear: No other sign of the zodiac is so concerned with the cycles of life.

The Scorpion's Score

➤ How many Scorpions does it take to screw in a light bulb?

➤ None. They like it in the dark.

Scorps are intense. They're dealing, after all, with life and death—and, by extension, with birth and sex. Scorpions are all about mystery, about how that poison stinger can so quickly change life into death, and Scorps can be both penetrating and incisive. Scorpio is one of the signs that has two rulers, Pluto and Mars. That's why this sign can be quite a warrior, and very powerful. Combined with their fixed nature, these people never give up!

Like all water signs, Scorps are more concerned with feelings than appearances, but as a fixed sign, they're often resistant to change as well. Scorps' ability to see through others' facades can serve them well, and they can wait forever for the right moment to get even or make their move.

Scorps are constantly probing beneath the obvious face of things, seeking what lies beneath. One of their rulers is Pluto, the invisible planet that rules beginnings and ends, both of which, like Pluto itself, occur out of natural sight.

Scorpions' intensity and probing may make them sound humorless and frightening, but these same characteristics create both passion and excitement as well. You may feel as if a Scorpion is looking right through you, but the feeling may be an invigorating one!

The Best and Worst of Scorpions

Scorps use what many astrologers call Scorpionic power to achieve their ends. But maybe we should just look at that power itself, because Scorpio is the zodiac's most powerful sign.

In pop astrology, you'll often find this power called sex, and yes, Scorpios do have a strongly developed sexuality. Sometimes, though, they may disguise this even from themselves, in which case they may constantly be seeking something they can't quite name.

Sometimes Scorps sublimate this energy into other projects, and they may be very aware of doing it. At their worst, they may choose to use their magnetism to coerce others in fanatical ways, such as Scorpio Charles Manson!

At their best, Scorpios are magnetic leaders, like Billy Graham: shrewd, faith-inspiring, compassionate, and brave. At their worst, they're manipulative, vengeful, or even cruel. Like the nuclear energy that shares Pluto's rule, they can use their power for good or evil, and Scorps would do well to use their tremendous energy and power in positive ways, such as healing and learning control.

Scorpio appears in the zodiac at a time when the earth seems to be dying: leaves fall from the trees; hibernating animals retreat to their caves; even humans go inside their houses and sit by their fires. But this retreat is in reality a regeneration, a rebirth, and this is the true source of Scorpio's power. In Scorpio's case, still waters really do run deep!

Scorp in Love

While Scorps may know everyone else's heart of hearts, they'll seldom reveal their own. When they do, though, they'll also be sharing a depth of passion no other sign can. Like their relatives the spiders, Scorps will weave a web of romance, attracting partners with their intricacy and magnetism. But they're also quick to retreat if they feel threatened—and once Scorps have hidden, it may be hard to get them to reveal themselves again.

You'd also do well not to injure a Scorp in love; their vengeance has a long memory and a fierce sting!

Don't forget that Scorpio is a water sign—sometimes emotional, sometimes moody, always slow to commit but very loyal once they do. Other water signs may be the most comfortable match for Scorp romance—Scorp may see other signs' approaches to love with too much clarity for romance.

Earth signs, like Taurus, Virgo, and Capricorn—fed by water—can do very well with Scorps. And Taurus is Scorps' opposite, as well, very sensuous and pleasure-loving, an interesting match for Scorpio's intensity.

The Healthy Scorp

Retentive Scorps may be prone to urinary tract infections or constipation, so reluctant are they to let anything out in the open. But they also have the potential to be great healers, not just of themselves but of others, because of their strong regenerative and transformative powers.

Healthy Scorps pay attention to their dreams, for both their informative and their imaginative power, and they should pay attention to what they eat and drink as well: Scorps' intake can truly make a big difference in how they feel. Any relaxation techniques that help Scorps get rid of old resentments and anger could also help them feel their best. But Scorps' most important health lesson is to let go—of repressed jealousy, anger, and resentment.

Scorps need to get adequate amounts of zinc or zinc supplements in their diets. This is essential for the growth, development, and functioning of the reproductive organs and prostate gland, as well as the general healing process, both important for Scorps.

Scorp at Home

Because Scorps require power and control, life at home can be full of struggles—power struggles! Or it can be a place where Scorps keep "everyone in line" until they get married and have children. Then it may not be so easy! But no matter what the kids or spouse do, Scorps are ready to defend them with their lives and stingers if necessary. Loyalty is very important to them.

When Scorps are unhappy, though, they head off to be alone—and heaven help you if you disturb them! Scorps usually need and want time alone regularly, to process their intense feelings. Without time alone, it can become very hard for Scorps to maintain their sense of control. For this reason, Scorps need their own hiding place at home, where no one else will bother them. This isn't just a corner in a room, either, but an entire room just for them—their space.

When Scorps are able to control themselves instead of others, they are very loving, loyal, and can give a great deal of themselves to their families and mates.

Scorp at Work

Scorps thrive on change, and a career that requires any renovation or strategy works very well for them. They may find creative outlets for their transformative energies, or they may be in the healing arts as doctors or counselors. Scorps also can do very well in fields like research or science—anything requiring that penetrating, probing eye will benefit from a Scorp touch.

Written in the Skies

Scorps are focused on regeneration and rebirth! Thousands of years ago, Scorpio was associated with sorcery and study of the mysteries that increased personal energy, such as tantric energy. This sign isn't always comfortable in our present society, where feelings and emotions are often disowned and disliked.

Scorps also are often involved in cleaning up waste or reviving the environment in some way. Scorpio is involved in eliminating toxins and regeneration, and that's why they excel at these jobs.

As the most powerful zodiac sign, Scorps also do well in any position where they can wield that power, be it management, finance, or directing. But that power also means that any field Scorps choose will benefit from their influence: even the seemingly meaningless is transformed once a Scorp is in charge.

Scorps and Their Money

Here again Scorps' retentive ways come to the forefront, and a Scorp and her money are not soon parted. Scorps also understand the dynamics of power and money, and their conservative approach pays off here as well.

Scorps will amass cash quietly in the background and then use it to achieve their ends. Outward appearances mean little to Scorps; to them, it's all about control and transformation, and they'll apply their money only where they feel it's necessary.

Sagittarius, the Archer: Seeking Life's Meanings

The Ninth Zodiac Sign

Sagittarius, the Archer ♐	November 22nd–December 22nd
Element:	Fire
Quality:	Mutable
Energy:	*Yang*
Ruler:	Jupiter
Color:	Purple
Gem:	Turquoise
Anatomy:	Liver, hips, and thighs
Keywords:	Understanding, enthusiasm, exploration
Mythological Archetypes:	Diana the Hunter, The Centaur
Celeb Archers:	Louisa May Alcott, Woody Allen, Kim Basinger, Walt Disney, Sinead O'Connor, Mark Twain

In Greek mythology, the best and bravest hunter was a woman—and her name was Diana (also Artemis). Protector of the wild animals, Diana was the guardian of all women as well, and whenever a woman died quickly and painlessly, she was said to have been slain by one of Diana's arrows.

The Archer's Point

➤ How many Sagittariuses does it take to screw in a light bulb?

➤ One, and eleven other signs to revolve around him.

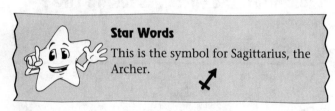

Star Words

This is the symbol for Sagittarius, the Archer.

The Archer's arrow searches for meaning, and Sagittarius can be thought of as the gypsy, the student, and the philosopher, all rolled into one. No other sign is so focused on finding life's basic truth. Archers burn with this need to understand, and, as a mutable sign, they thrive on the changes this search can provide.

Archers are a yang sign, too, so they're always moving toward more and more experience. This is a party sign, and the party is marked by the fire sign's enthusiasm, high spirits, and a whole lot of fun. Archers' optimism is contagious, and their honesty and directness can be a breath of fresh air.

Archers are ruled by Jupiter, the king of the Roman gods, and the planet of good fortune, optimism, expansion, and abundance. (The word "jovial" is a derivative of the Latin form of Jupiter.) Jupiter is a fortunate ruler, and Archers tend to be freedom-loving, energetic people.

Another Archer myth is that of the centaur, half human, half beast. You may remember them in living color, prancing and galloping around during Beethoven's 6th Symphony in *Fantasia*—and that's not a bad picture of centaur life: one big party! But remember that half of the centaur is human, and hence thinking and searching for meaning and truth, like an Archer!

The Best and Worst of Archers

Archers thrive on and freedom, and they never tire of a change of scenery. Sure, they may forget your date or miss that important deadline, but they're always the life of the party, and just plain fun!

Archers' enthusiasm is bound to be contagious, but their lack of commitment can annoy other more responsible signs. Their generosity may spill into excessiveness; their optimism may make them blind to details; and their honesty can make their remarks sound blunt or inconsiderate. But the carefree adventurousness of Sagittarius can be a welcome change.

Most dangerous to Archers can be their tendency toward dogma. Because they're seeking a universal truth rather than an individual one, they may mistake a trend for that truth and then become rather preachy about its powers. But Archers truly do wish to unite all people under one idea, and if they believe they've found it, they're eager to share it with all.

Still, for Archers, it's the getting there that's more than half the fun: Archers love travel, new places, and seeking. Go along for the ride if you dare—and if you're an Archer yourself, you won't think twice!

Archers in Love

Commitment? Sure. Just don't expect it to go on too long! Mutable Archers are always on the move, and if they do find their true love, they may have left a bevy of admirers behind, trying in vain to find their tracks.

Love is fun! Romance is a gas! Passion is excitement! See how Sagittarius breeds exclamation points? Those who require loyalty and longevity in love might do well to look elsewhere, but if you're looking for a good time, call 1-800-ARCHER.

Archers aren't just looking for a good time, although that's part of it: they want a trail-mate for their journey. They're here to seek, and householders aren't particularly interested in living a life on the trail. It takes a special person to want to adventure off with a Sag; the future is so open to possibilities, but also so unsettled. This isn't the person you want if you're after a mate to "settle down" with. But for another adventurer, a Sag is a great journeyer.

Archers aren't concerned with details, which means they can drive more detail-oriented signs like Virgo to distraction. And Archers expect that everyone will want to have as much fun as they do, which tends to leave Scorpio and Taurus back in the dust, too. Archers will do best with other fire signs, where the romance can be both fiery and adventurous. Just don't forget that air feeds fire, too: Gemini, Libra, and Aquarius may have just the kind of surprises that Archers love!

The Healthy Archer

Energetic Archers can sometimes forget to slow down. And while they're galloping along, they may be gathering more and more new projects before they've finished any they've already started. All this running can make them prone to nervous exhaustion or just plain confusion. Sometimes it's necessary for racing-ahead Archers to STOP.

Sagittarius rules the hips, thighs, and liver, all of which can be severely harmed by overindulgence. Archers would do well to work on exercises that help them stay centered physically, and this, in turn, will help them not to lose sight of the big picture they envision.

Archers need to be aware of the problems of excess sugar, fat, or even alcohol; all can harm their livers. Too much overindulgence in these foods can really slow them down and make them sick. Archers need adequate amounts of vitamin K, inositol, manganese, and molybdenum to maintain normal liver function and metabolize fats. Detoxifying their liver around mid-life also can prevent major health problems later.

Archers at Home

Archers are great entertainers, and everyone loves a party at Archer's house. Yes, they may forget to serve—or to make—a main course, but all will be having too much fun to care.

You won't often find children at Archer's house, though. This adventurous sign doesn't want to be tied down. Archers like to feel free to set out for the next adventure, and home can just as easily be a tent in the Serengeti or on Mt. Denali, as a bachelor pad in the French Quarter or on Beale Street.

But wherever Archer's tent is pitched, you can be sure that's where you'll find the action.

Archers at Work

Because Archers tend to lose interest before a project is completed, it's best to have them on your idea team. Archers do well, though, in all areas of communications, or anywhere a sense of humor and excitement are needed— and they may be clowns, tricksters, or even court jesters! They'll also do well as *National Geographic* photographers —or any kind of photographer.

Archers also can be found in positions that require risk, from the stock market to test piloting. They may be gamblers—Archers believe in their luck, and that optimism really does make them lucky.

Archers are often found in education, medicine, the legal system, foreign relations, the travel industry, or traveling for business, such as importers/exporters, or in sales. Archers tend to be highly educated and very well read; Sagittarius often produces philosophers, preachers, or anyone associated with inspiring others. One of the best-known Archers at work was Gene Roddenberry, the creator of *Star Trek*. Roddenberry created a crew that included a black woman, a Russian, an Asian, and an alien! Old *Star Treks* may look dated now, but back then, Roddenberry's vision was truly revolutionary.

Archers and Their Money

Because they're more interested in the big picture than the little details, Archers may forget that they borrowed that $20 from you as soon as they've got it in their hand. And their irresponsibility with money may irk their more dependable friends to no end. But those same dependable friends will always come through for Archers—and, because Archers know it, they don't sweat it.

Out of Orbit

Over-confident Archers may tend to over-extend themselves—and their resources—for the sake of a good time, but here again their luck comes into play: Archers will put their last $100 on that 50-to-one shot—and it'll come in!

As a mutable sign, Archers can be very resourceful, so they're able to scrape something together, even if they're broke. Of course that could lead back to borrowing from others. Very resourceful of them!

Chapter 9

The Elder, the Rebel, and the Healer: Capricorn, Aquarius, and Pisces Sun Signs

Perhaps no three signs are more different than the signs of winter: Capricorn, Aquarius, and Pisces. Capricorn is the organized, goal-setting achiever; Aquarius is the inventive, humanitarian revolutionary; and Pisces is the compassionate, all-understanding healer.

Capricorn, the Goat: Ain't No Mountain High Enough

The Tenth Zodiac Sign

Capricorn the Goat ♑	December 22nd–January 21st
Element:	Earth
Quality:	Cardinal
Energy:	*Yin*
Ruler:	Saturn
Color:	Brown
Gem:	Garnet
Anatomy:	Bones, joints, and knees
Keywords:	Achievement, structure, organization
Mythological Archetype:	Father Time, Cronus
Celeb Goats:	Muhammad Ali, Joan of Arc, Martin Luther King, Jr., Mary Tyler Moore, Elvis Presley, Howard Stern

Goat Tales

➤ How many Capricorns does it take to screw in a light bulb?

➤ One, but it has to be her idea.

No sign's public persona is closer to its values than a Goat's, and no sign is more directed toward its goals. Intense and practical, Goats will bide their time, waiting for the right moment to climb that peak, because once they do, they intend to stay there.

Self-control, of both will and emotion, helps Goats achieve their aims. As the cardinal earth sign, Goat is decidedly down to earth in its efforts, and, with its *yin* energy, a Goat uses the mind rather than physical force to reach its goals.

But Capricorn isn't just any goat; it's a sea-goat, and, as a creature that's half-fish, it also can use water's deeper powers to its advantage. Ultimately, though, Goats' goals are always down-to-earth, so, no matter what their means to get there, their ends are always practical and constructive.

Star Words
This is the symbol for Capricorn, the Goat.

Capricorn is society's "elder." Goats are here to accept responsibilities for helping others and building a society that meets the needs of the people. They also want to build something stable and enduring—after all, this sign is ruled by Saturn, also known as Father Time.

Goats are meant to create a balance between responsible nurturing and meeting the responsibilities of being the elders. People don't become elders when they're young, though, so Goats understand the patience required to learn what's important.

The Best and Worst of Goats

It can be lonely at the top, but if Goats want to be there, they'll have to learn to live with solitude. At their best, Goats are ambitious, organized, efficient, and responsible, but Goats also can be cold, calculating, suspicious, and rigid.

In their effort to achieve security, Goats may step on anything, or anyone, that stands in their way. But they can be surprisingly kind, too, especially to those who have done them favors or kindnesses. Goats are motivated by pride; they don't like to be beholden, and they'll repay favors generously.

Goats' practicality can be a welcome asset in the cold of winter: the logs will be stacked ready next to the door, and the cupboard will be filled with all that's needed to get through the cold months. And Goats will surprise you, too, with their quiet, dry wit helping to pass the winter nights.

Written in the Skies

It's cold at the start of winter, and Capricorn's a cold sign—cold and calculating. Unlike another climber, the Ram, the Goats' steps are slow and sure: Goats want to make sure they get where they're going, so they're careful to take their time. With their energy turned inward, toward self-control, Goats quietly and steadily work toward their goals. And ruled by practical Saturn, they're bound to get there, too.

Goats in Love

Goats seek their approval from the world-at-large, which may make personal relationships seem secondary to them, but once you discover Goats' dry sense of humor, you'll find a way to their hearts as well.

When you penetrate that icy reserve, in fact, you'll find the possibilities for deep love and strong loyalty. With their deepest feelings buried beneath the surface, Goats protect those they care for, and they'll stick around when the going gets tough.

Stability matters more to Goats than to any other sign, so when it comes to romance, they'll seek comfort over pleasure, and longevity over romance. Goats do well with other earth signs, but it can be with water signs that the best connections may occur: a nurturing Cancer, passionate Scorpio, or sympathetic Pisces may help a Goat to grow in new ways.

The Healthy Goat

Goats can be pessimistic, and they need to beware of the melancholy that pessimism can bring. But cautious Goats often live long, long lives: Helena Rubinstein, Albert Schweitzer, and Carl Sandburg lived well into their 90s, for example. What seems to shorten Goats' lives most often is their potential power: both Joan of Arc and Martin Luther King, Jr. were Goats, after all.

Many Goat afflictions are due to too much rigidity in their thinking or behavior: the difficulty of representing tradition is getting too rigid about it! Eventually this can translate into arthritis or rheumatism.

As for vitamins, what else? Goats need calcium to build those bones and teeth, as well as to keep their nerves under control. Goats also need plenty of vitamin C, which is necessary for forming skin, ligaments, bones, healthy teeth, and gums. And they need to get enough vitamin D and magnesium for utilizing the calcium to build their bones.

Capricorn rules the skeleton, bones, and teeth—all the *structural* aspects of the body that Goats are associated with. For this reason, alternative therapies that deal with the structure of the body, such as chiropractic or Feldenkrais, a form of structural and physical therapy, are very appropriate for Goats.

Goats at Home

Our favorite Goats seem to understand the importance of a place of their own, a quiet, private retreat from all the trappings that can come with power. Here they'll have their favorite music playing, their favorite pictures on the walls, and their favorite books stacked up next to their favorite chair.

Like all earth signs, Goats appreciate the comforts of home, but they're more likely to use it as a getaway than a base of operations. Goats know the importance of strong foundations, and their home will be warm and secure, a haven from those cold winter storms.

And have you heard the one about Cronus (another name for Saturn, Capricorn's ruler), who ate his children, because he was certain one of them was going to overthrow him? Talk about being rigid and sticking to tradition! Fortunately, his wife substituted a rock for one of the kids, who just happened to be Zeus, also known as Jupiter. Jupiter later went on to lead his brothers and sisters, who were freed (alive) from their father's stomach, in what seems to be a justified revolt against their father!

Goats at Work

Goats like to be in charge, and if they don't start there, it's usually where they'll end up. Rags-to-riches Goats abound, such as Howard Hughes and Aristotle Onassis, as well as powerful Goats, like Mao Tse-tung and Joseph Stalin.

The older Goats get, the more rewarding their lives are likely to become. Once they've achieved the power they've sought, they can relax with the wisdom they've gained and the lessons they can share with others. Many Goats live long lives as writers or artists, including J. R. R. Tolkein, Alfred Stieglitz, and Anton Chekhov. And Goats are found in business, where there are a lot of mountains to climb. As Goats are very achievement-oriented, they reach the top of many fields!

Written in the Skies

More Presidents of the United States have been born with their Sun or Moon in Capricorn than any other sign. Why? Because Goats' ambitions, shrewdness, and slow, steady movement toward their goals are just what are required for executive positions. Goats aspire to the top spot, and they get there, too!

Goats and Their Money

Goats understand the power that can come with money, and, as a cardinal sign, they're likely to do things with it in order to turn it into even more money—buying, selling, and making deals. Goats use their money to attain and maintain power: money means control to a Goat, and control and power are Goats' driving forces. They also are generous with their money once they have it, but the generosity is tied to their power and prestige: Goats truly understand the phrase, "Money talks."

Aquarius, the Water Bearer: The Inventive Individual

The Eleventh Zodiac Sign

Aquarius, the Water Bearer ≈	January 21st–February 19th
Element:	Air
Quality:	Fixed
Energy:	*Yang*

continues

The Eleventh Zodiac Sign...continued

Rulers:	Uranus and Saturn
Color:	Violet
Gem:	Amethyst
Anatomy:	Ankles and circulation
Keywords:	Humanitarian, unique, revolutionary
Mythological Archetypes:	Deucalion and Pyrrha, Noah's Ark
Celeb W-Bs:	Susan B. Anthony, Wolfgang Amadeus Mozart, Paul Newman, Vanessa Redgrave, Virginia Woolf, Boris Yeltsin

Water-Bearer Wonders

➤ How many Aquarians does it take to screw in a light bulb?

➤ One, and he has to use the latest technology to do it.

Aquarius is where you'll find the zodiac's eccentric individualists and crazy inventors. Anything out of the ordinary interests this independent sign, and Water Bearers are often trend spotters and trendsetters.

Water Bearers' fixed air represents persistent development of the intellect through communication, and their planetary influence, Uranus, means they'll be committed to innovation and change. Aquarians will often be progressive and open-minded, but that fixed quality means they'll often be fixed in their opinions as well.

Water Bearers will do anything to avoid boredom, and they care little for what others think, especially once they've determined their own particular cause. Their ambition is for humankind rather than just themselves, and you'll find some of the great progressive thinkers here: Charles Darwin, Abraham Lincoln, Thomas Edison, and Franklin Delano Roosevelt, for example.

Star Words

This is the symbol for Aquarius, the Water Bearer.

♒

Most W-Bs find Earth to be a very dense place! Most of them are 50 years or more ahead of their time, and talking to the rest of us can seem like a difficult and laborious process. Aquarians often feel like they're visiting from another planet, because their ideas are so advanced. Trouble is, sometimes they forget their missions once they get here and find out how dense this place really is!

So why is it that Aquarius, the Water Bearer, is an air sign, not a water sign? Good question. But look at this sign's symbol, ♒, to find your answer. This water is in the form of waves, which are caused by wind: the motion of air on water. These wavy lines also represent the serpents of knowledge; the parts of the body ruled by Aquarius, the ankles and the circulatory system; and lightning that cleans air and leaves that "ozone buzz." Remember that this name doesn't refer to the water itself but to its carrier: Aquarius is the "water bearer," the most human of the signs.

Among the myths associated with the sign of Aquarius are the great deluge myths: Noah's Ark in the Judeo-Christian tradition and Deucalion and Pyrrha in the Greek tradition. After surviving the Greek deluge by building a wooden box to float in, Deucalion and Pyrrha created a new race of people by throwing rocks over their shoulders: the rocks that Deucalion threw became men, and the rocks that Pyrrha threw became women.

The Best and Worst of W-B

Idealistic, inventive, and original, W-Bs can all-too-easily seem aloof, detached, or just plain cranky. In fact, W-Bs' tendency to go against the grain can separate them from other people, even the more abstract "humanity" they are trying to help.

More than any other sign, W-Bs have a human connection, and they seek to bring all humans together without regard for any of the imaginary divisions humans themselves have created. This same disregard for human difference, though, may leave W-Bs without any close relationships of their own.

W-Bs' strongest trait is their intellectual independence, their refusal to be pigeonholed. W-Bs really do hear a "different drummer," and it may even be they who are playing those drums! W-Bs can be radicals, renegades, or bohemians too, but depending on other factors in the chart, this may not be obvious. They can look perfectly normal yet have very different ideas. So even though they may pass for one of us, they don't *feel* like us.

It's almost as though they're aliens from another star system, living in human bodies. W-Bs often experiment with or observe friends, mates, or partners, just to see what they will do under a particular set of circumstances, and they can be very detached about this process—although the results may be enough to keep them interested in a person!

W-Bs in Love

Independent W-Bs need partners who understand that independence and who won't feel threatened by it, and in return they'll offer their partners the same kind of freedom. With the right partner, W-Bs will be constant and true: remember, this is a fixed sign, reluctant to change once it's established what it considers the right path.

Some W-Bs may sacrifice personal relationships to pursue a greater good, and some may seem aloof even in the best of relationships. Sometimes W-Bs' relationships themselves will become laboratories for their creativity, as they did in the cases of James Joyce, Federico Fellini, Gertrude Stein, and W. Somerset Maugham. W-Bs are always seeking what's best for humankind, and they may sometimes lose sight of individual humans in the process.

Air signs—Gemini, Libra, other Aquarians—will naturally combine well with Aquarius, but pay attention to the fire-feeding capabilities of air, too: the innovation of a W-B may be just what Aries, Leo, or Sag needs for some mutual excitement.

The Healthy W-B

The ankles and the circulatory system are ruled by Aquarius: the ankles supporting our ability to stand, and circulation the movement of our very lifeblood through our bodies. W-Bs are the very essence of human existence, and it's important that in their tendency to think and see globally, they don't lose sight of these areas closer to home.

Vitamins and, of course, eating right can keep W-Bs at their fittest. W-Bs need magnesium—and plenty of it—in their diets to keep their circulation and heart (Leo is their opposite) in good shape. Magnesium also is needed for the electrical charges that move nutrients in and out of cells, as well as for absorbing and using vitamins and minerals.

W-Bs may heal well with acupuncture or chiropractic, because Saturn is their coruler and these healing techniques deal with the nervous system and their energy. Exercise also plays an important role; with their heads in the clouds, W-Bs may forget that they have a body to take care of as well!

W-Bs hold the mind and spirit in high esteem, but they need to pay attention to what connects them to the rest of humanity, too, and to keep their lifeblood circulating freely.

W-Bs at Home

W-Bs' home is the world, and they populate that world with a variety of people, especially the unusual, the eccentric, and those who are just plain different. "Live and let live" is a W-B motto, and they'll open their doors to anyone who needs their shelter. W-Bs believe that they can change people's lives just by being a part of them, and if their homes sometimes resemble Noah's Arks of humanity, it's no coincidence.

Even though they may seem aloof, W-B's individual goals are always based on a greater good. This holds true at home, too: altruistic and giving, W-Bs share their homes with all.

W-Bs at Work

Clever, original W-Bs can excel in any profession in which creativity is a plus. This isn't limited just to the arts, either, but can extend to scientific innovation and invention, to public service or civil rights reform, even to owning a business of their own or marketing someone else's unique ideas. Many also work in broadcast media.

W-Bs understand that the future is where innovation lies, and their careers may often lead others toward that future. Charles Lindbergh was a W-B, for example, and so is Ronald Reagan. W-Bs also may be geniuses within their chosen field, like golfer Jack Nicklaus or dancer Mikhail Baryshnikov.

W-Bs can be revolutionaries, sometimes associated with actual government revolutions, like Boris Yeltsin and Angela Davis, and often associated with ideas, causes, or inventions that eventually revolutionize the world.

But no matter where they work, you can count on W-Bs to be the ones on the cutting edge, the ones with ideas, the ones with creative solutions to the problems everyone else thought insoluble.

W-Bs and Their Money

W-Bs are givers rather than keepers, and, with their vision focused on the future, they're not likely to concern themselves with the here and now. This can translate into a disregard for money, including a tendency to go beyond their budgets or overextend themselves in other ways.

With their vision for the future, though, W-Bs can potentially do well in speculative ventures, especially in areas that will be using new technology. Well-selected investments in these areas now can protect W-Bs moving into their more uncertain futures.

Pisces, the Fishes: Dream Weavers

The Twelfth Zodiac Sign

Pisces, the Fishes ♓	February 19th–March 21st
Element:	Water
Quality:	Mutable
Energy:	*Yin*
Rulers:	Neptune and Jupiter
Color:	Sea-Green
Gem:	Aquamarine
Anatomy:	Feet, immune system, hormonal system

continues

The Twelfth Zodiac Sign...continued

Keywords:	Compassion, universality, inclusiveness
Mythological Archetype:	The Healer, Christ
Celeb Fishes:	Elizabeth Barrett Browning, Johnny Cash, Billy Crystal, Mikhail Gorbachev, Liza Minnelli, Ralph Nader, Elizabeth Taylor

Fish Facts

➤ How many Pisces does it take to screw in a light bulb?

➤ The light went out?

Star Words

This is the symbol for Pisces, the Fishes.

♓

True to the Piscean paradox, here's a symbol ♓ with multiple meanings. It represents two fishes tied together; a picture of the human feet, which Pisces rules; or two crescent moons, connected by a straight line—emotion and higher consciousness tied down to the material world. No wonder Fishes so often feel misunderstood and yet have so many possibilities—even their symbol is all-encompassing!

Mutable water: from solid (ice) to liquid to gas (vapor). This is the character of Pisces, changing according to outside conditions. And yet Fishes live largely in the world of the imagination, the realm of dreams, where objects and events seem to have no connection to outer reality. What's going on here?

rooted. As in all areas, though, Fishes need to beware of those who would take advantage of them: they're quick to trust, and all too easily hurt.

Healthy Fishes

Fishes can tend to overindulge, and need to be careful to limit their intake of everything from bread to wine. Fishes may be overweight or have a tendency to retain water. In addition, Pisces rules the feet, and Fishes should take particular care to avoid sprains, or even breaks, to that sensitive area.

Fishes don't always take care of themselves as well as they do others, but one way to start would be through a holistic fitness regimen that takes into account both body and soul. One vitamin that can help Fishes feel their best is pantothenic acid, which helps stimulate their adrenal glands and increase their immune systems. Because Pisces appears to rule the immune system, all aids to this system—like astragalus or echinacea herbs—are helpful for Fishes.

Pisces also seems to be in charge of hormones, so keeping these in balance may be very important. Fishes are very sensitive to foods and poisons in their environment, and may need to be detoxified more frequently than any other. Alcohol and drugs are very difficult for them to process; even prescription drugs can wreak havoc on their bodies, so it's very important for Fishes to watch their intake and notice the changes in their body.

At Home

Fishes use their homes as places for spiritual renewal—or abuse. Just as they may swim with or against the current, they may use their homes as refuges or dens of iniquity, and the choice they make will spill over into other areas of their life as well.

This last sign creates the possibility to move beyond self into transcendence, represented to humans as the world of dreams and faith. But this also can be a world of sheer escapism, where dreaming is done for its own sake. Fishes, we could say, can either sink or swim.

Put another way, Fishes know which way the river is running and may swim with it or against it. Swimming against it can mean they may find a way to another stream ("hooked" Fishes can channel their addictions, for example), while swimming with it may mean, quite literally, "going with the flow," and living intuitively.

Fishes are highly intuitive, in fact, and Pisces is the sign that merges with others so easily that these people don't always know what's theirs and what belongs to someone else. Fishes are frequently so sensitive to the vibrations of others that they can go into work and instantly feel how others are doing. Unfortunately, they also may unconsciously take responsibility for how others are doing, or wonder why they feel so bad—especially when they woke up feeling so good!

For this reason, fishes can have a hard time maintaining their boundaries and knowing what *they're* feeling, as opposed to what others are feeling. The reason for this boundary stuff goes back to the main point of Pisces, which is to merge with others—and eventually the Source or God. Fishes are in a highly spiritual sign, living in a very nonspiritual world. For this reason it's easy for them to get off-track by merging with the wrong people and to get away from their true spiritual focus.

Above all, Fishes are here to give, not just to those like themselves, but to anyone that needs their help, love, attention, or whatever. Have you ever watched *The X Files*? Mulder is probably a Pisces, or else he has a strong Neptune! After all, his poster reads: "I want to believe."

Pisces is associated with baptism, spiritual cleansing, and renewal, and Venus is "exalted" here, which means that the love and beauty she rules are of a universal rather than a personal nature. Fishes are a symbol of divine purity; in fact, the birth of Christ is associated with the beginning of the Age of Pisces.

The Best and Worst of Fishes

Compassionate Fishes can see deep into the human psyche, probe the depths of emotions, lend a sympathetic ear, or play an intuitive hunch. But they can also be oh-so-sad, shy, timid, or just plain impractical. Fishes can seem both lazy and over talkative, the talk seeming to go on and on about any number of unlikely possibilities.

But Fishes can change, too, and change can be good: it can mean adaptability. Because of their extraordinary sensitivity, Fishes are often creative artistically, and their understanding of people sometimes seems limitless (though the understanding doesn't always extend to themselves).

Out of Orbit

Impressionable Fishes can fall for just about any hard-luck story; dreamers themselves, they can easily get caught up in the dreams of others as well. Fishes can tend toward addiction, too, whether in food, alcohol, drugs, or simply the wrong kinds of people. Sometimes, in fact, their lives can seem filled with trouble.

Pisces is the sign that represents spirituality—not religion, like Sagittarius—but a true need to have a relationship with a higher power. When these spiritual needs aren't fulfilled, Fishes become involved in the negative side of

this energy, which is escapism. That's where the drugs, alcohol, or sugar addictions come in, as well as the wrong kinds of people.

Fishes need to learn to live by faith and intuition: once they do this, they're on the right track. Einstein was a Pisces, and his theories were "impractical," but correct. Doe the universe need dreamers and people that can transcer the boundaries of normal reality? And does that make them impractical? Or just different from the rest of us?

Fishes often channel their imagination and creativity the arts: Michelangelo was a Pisces, and so were Ren and Chopin. Fishes do best when they believe in th selves and their dreams the same way they believe ers' dreams—but this isn't always an easy task!

Fishes in Love

Kind, perceptive, sensitive Fishes look at the in others, at the essence rather than the surface. truly seeking their soul mates, the most profo possible and so may be disappointed when r to live up to their idealistic expectations.

Fishes in love can create an enchanting pl happens, a space separate from the rest of Fishes and their loved ones alone. Fishes can translate that feeling, too: you'll alv you're the object of Fishes' affection.

Water, water, water: of course Fishes Cancers, Scorpios, and other Pisces. where empathy can go far—if Fishe flighty signs like Gemini, Libra, an Fishes swimming in their wake— heights of awareness. Fishes can nurturing earth signs, and earth keep Fishes' tendency toward f

If Fishes find true love, they're more likely to create a home as refuge, and Fishes would do well to create their own hidden cave, a place to renew themselves, to meditate, and to be introspective—retreat can bring healthy renewal.

Fishes at Work

Because Fishes love to combine their real life with their imaginary one, they can often be found in the world of theater or film, or in any of the arts. But they also can do quite well in business or even politics, where their sensitivity can give them powerful insights less intuitive signs might miss.

Fishes like to work behind the scenes or alone: fame and recognition aren't what drive them. Because of this, Fishes can be great manipulators or builders. Or they may be photographers—beautifully capturing others' spirits on film.

Fishes are often found, too, in areas where their capabilities for the spiritual can be used: they may be astrologers or monks, religious leaders or healers. Fishes are known for their ability to sacrifice themselves for others.

Pisces also deals with images, so these people are gifted at leading others through visualization experiences and meditations and bringing people to a higher level of awareness and consciousness. Above all, Fishes are here to help the rest of us transcend our normal ruts, beliefs, and boundaries, and see the illusions we live under.

Fishes and Their Money

Here again, Fishes need to be wary of others' stories: they're all too easily convinced to hand over their life savings to help a friend (or anyone) they think is in need. Money can swim in and out of Fishes' lives as mysteriously as everything and everyone else does, and impractical Fishes don't always understand why.

Because they're not really prone to moneymaking enterprises themselves, Fishes' money may come from outside sources, and it may go back outside, too. Many Fishes work in the service sector, so they may not get the kind of money that business enterprises pay. But what Fishes *are* good at are the dreams where all good ideas—including potential moneymaking ones—begin. Here's a sign whose intuitive hunches are always worth pursuing.

Chapter 10

Moon Phases and the Natural World

In This Chapter

➤ Waxing and waning: the phases of the Moon

➤ The effect of Moon phases on our daily lives

➤ Beware of the void-of-course Moon

Chances are you're already aware of the Moon's *phases*, even if you've never paid them much attention. In its $29\frac{1}{2}$-day cycle, the Moon moves through four major phases: the New Moon, the First Quarter Moon, the Full Moon, and the Last Quarter Moon.

In this chapter we'll explore just how the Moon affects everything and everyone here on Earth.

Star Words

Moon phases are the names for the eight parts of the Moon's 29¹/₂-day cycle. They are: the New Moon, Crescent Moon, First Quarter Moon, Gibbous Moon, Full Moon, Disseminating Moon, Last Quarter Moon, and the Balsamic Moon.

Waxing and Waning: The Phases of the Moon

How much of the Moon is illuminated—and therefore, what phase we see—depends upon its angle to the Sun. The Moon begins *waxing*, or growing in light, at the New Moon until it's a Full Moon. Then the Moon begins to *wane*, or decrease in light, at the Full Moon until the next New Moon.

Star Words

A waxing Moon grows in light from the New Moon to the Full Moon. A *waning Moon* decreases in light from the Full Moon until the next New Moon.

Here on Earth, we see these changes in the Moon's appearance. As it moves through these phases, the Moon is moving through the signs as well, spending about 2¹/₂ days in each sign.

The Moon travels about one degree every two hours—sometimes faster or slower—which translates into crossing a sign about every 60 hours. And, the Moon's energies are manifested differently in each of the signs. The 29¹/₂-day cycle of the Moon—from New Moon to New Moon—is how we got our month. And Monday is named for the Moon, too.

Then there's *a void-of-course Moon,* one that has made its last major aspect to other planets until it moves into the next sign. This is a period when it's best not to begin things: purchases can turn out to be mistakes or bad investments, decisions can be the wrong ones, and new starts or actions taken tend to come to nothing. While you can't always delay decisions, it's best to be aware of these periods in order to avoid what could be costly mistakes.

Out of Orbit

When the Moon is void of course, its energy is spent, and this is a time of gestation, research, or rest. Either nothing will come of decisions made during this time, or there will be unexpected problems that can prevent a successful completion.

Hitler's non-aggression pact with Russia and the Vietnam Peace Accord are two examples of treaties signed during a void-of-course Moon. These Moon periods are associated with nothing coming of events, decisions, or agreements made during them. In the case of Hitler and Russia, we all know how that ended up: war. There was never any intention on Hitler's part to keep the agreement.

The Effect of Moon Phases on Our Daily Lives

Understanding the Moon's phases and their effect on our daily lives can help us work with these energies rather than against them. Let's take a walk through each to see exactly what this means.

A New Moon begins in darkness and will slowly emerge as a crescent that appears to us like the curve of the letter D. This is the Moon that is full of possibilities, the Moon of beginnings, as well as a period when people have a natural urge to start something.

The First Quarter, or Waxing, Moon, is also known as the Half Moon and appears to us as a filled-in D. This is the Moon that will see projects through, the Moon of action and independence. It also can bring external challenges to light, and in fact, the astrological definition of a First Quarter Moon is "crisis in action." It's typically a period when a lot is happening—and when there's often a crisis or challenge associated with whatever was started at the time of the New Moon.

The Moon is always exactly opposite the Sun when it is Full, and it's at this point that activities are brought to fruition, like a blossoming flower—whatever was being developed comes to light at this time. Everything's visible during a Full Moon, when it truly has become a "full circle."

The Last Quarter Moon looks like a filled-in C, and is the midpoint of the Moon's waning phase. It's a time to assess, to look over what's been accomplished, to learn from one's mistakes, and to wind down and prepare for the next cycle.

Written in the Skies

A Moon cycle, also known as a goddess cycle, can be viewed at its literal level—a woman's natural 28-day menstrual cycle. Or it can be taken to a more metaphoric level, such as birth—growth—aging—death—rebirth. Viewed metaphorically, we can see why the Moon rules everything from gardens to growth and from banquets to bath water.

During the Moon's dark night, which is called a Balsamic Moon, before it once again begins its next cycle, psychic energy is at its peak. It's time to retreat, to reflect, and to get ready to begin again.

The Moon has been a woman for as long as anyone can remember, and, with the recent resurgence of interest in goddesses and goddess cycles, the phases of the Moon have reclaimed their ancient stories as well.

Moon Signs Show the Way

Annual Moon sign guides, like *Llewellyn's Moon Sign Book*, show the best times for activities as diverse as getting your hair cut, borrowing money, having your teeth filled, getting married, and buying a house. Some of these guides, in fact, list the best and worst times for over 100 activities.

Basically, Moon sign guides will tell you things like the best time to buy a house is when the Moon is in a fixed sign (Taurus, Leo, Scorpio, or Aquarius), or that the best time to go fishing is when the Moon is in a water sign (Cancer, Scorpio, or Pisces). If you've been paying attention as we've gone along, you'll soon be making these connections on your own.

Once we learn to associate the Moon's natural cycles— both through its phases and through the signs—with our own, we can plan our lives to move *with* these rhythms rather than *against* them. For example, if you sow seeds (in other words, start something) during a waning Moon, the seeds will usually germinate more poorly than if you sow in a waxing Moon. If you weed in a waxing Moon, you may spread the weeds rather than destroy them.

The Elements and Their Corresponding Plant Organs

Element	Signs	Corresponding Plant Organs
Earth	Taurus, Virgo, Capricorn	Roots (earth = underground)
Air	Gemini, Libra, Aquarius	Flower (air = airborne pollen)
Fire	Aries, Leo, Sagittarius	Seed (fire = beginnings)
Water	Cancer, Scorpio, Pisces	Leaves and stems (water = growth)

Only the Beginning: The New Moon

The New Moon is the very beginning of everything—when a seed first germinates and comes out of its seed capsule and the first green shoots appear. This is life at its most basic, with only instinct to guide it, the starting point for all ventures. The Sun and Moon are conjunct, or in the same place, during a New Moon, so they'll have the same sign.

The New Moon is the most masculine form of the Moon's feminine energy, because this is its most active, primitive, and impulsive phase. This is a good time to begin new projects, or to set the plans you've made in motion. It's a good time to plant anything that you hope to see succeed, in fact.

You can think of the New Moon as the planted seed, the first of the elemental powers of fertility and nurturing. This Moon represents gestation, the first step toward birth. Aries is the sign associated with this Moon.

Challenges from Outside: The First Quarter Moon

During the First Quarter Moon, you'll begin to see a seedling's stem with its first pair of leaves, and it will have started to establish its root system. In the next phase—Gibbous Moon—it will make its first buds. This is the time to make sure that everything continues to go smoothly. Here is where you'll meet your challenges—in the case of that seedling, a late spring frost could threaten it, while in the case of a project, someone in power may question your direction or motive.

During this phase, the Moon is 90 degrees ahead of the Sun, or square to it, so it's a time of challenges and, hence, a good time to seek guidance. A seedling may flounder in the hot sun or strong wind, and you may need to stake it or give it more water. Or that project, gathering its own momentum, may run into the first bureaucratic snafu.

The key during a First Quarter Moon is to know that challenges will appear so that you can anticipate them, prepare, and meet them. This Moon is associated with Cancer, because nurturing is required to further programs, projects, and efforts.

All Lit Up: The Full Moon

When the Moon is full, it's exactly opposite the Sun, and in this bright glare, all activities reach their stage of fruition. This is the time when the flower blooms and you see the results of your efforts. If things haven't gone quite according to plan, everything that's wrong will suddenly be seen quite clearly, while, if they have, it will be the time to gather your rewards.

This is the Moon of high energy, the Moon's highest peak before it begins its waning phase. Crazy things happen during Full Moons, often because all that energy hasn't been channeled during the earlier phases.

A Full Moon can be a time of grand achievement or great disillusionment. This is the Moon most closely associated with Libra, or seeing things from other people's points of view. And this period is associated with rewards or disappointments, as this is when others become aware of what you're doing. If you followed the Moon's phases in your planning and development up to this point, you're probably enjoying the fruits of your labors.

Written in the Skies

What's a Blue Moon? And why do things only happen "Once in a Blue Moon"? Well, there are usually 13 full Moons each year, and, while the lunar cycle is about 29½ days, months are anywhere from 28 to 31 days. Once in a Blue Moon, there are 2 Full Moons during one month, and that second Full Moon is called the "Blue Moon."

Challenges from Inside: The Last Quarter Moon

Just because the Moon is continuing to wane doesn't mean its energies aren't at work; they're just moving in a different direction. Once again the Moon is 90 degrees from the Sun, though on the other side of the circle, and so the Last Quarter Moon is assessment time, when we look back at what we've done and see where we can make improvements. We'll also note what we did right, of course. But rather than bask in our glory, as we did during the Full Moon, it's best to use this time to diagnose and correct.

All this assessment can lead to disappointment or a resolve to improve or do better, both of which can in turn lead to internal challenges as we question whether we should have tackled something like this in the first place. And sometimes the Last Quarter Moon means we have to go back to square one and start all over again.

This is a good time to remember that mistakes are lessons, not reprimands. If you learn from your errors and don't repeat them, then you should congratulate yourself. And learning from your errors is what this Last Quarter Moon is all about.

The Last Quarter Moon is the Wise Woman, whose knowledge of the mystical and unknown can help us arrive at greater understanding. This is the Moon associated with Scorpio.

Finally, there's the Balsamic cycle, part of the Last Quarter cycle, the dark Moon when the plant releases its seed to start the next generation—the plants that will be born at the beginning of the next New Moon phase. This is the period that bridges the ending of the last cycle with the beginning of the one to come.

Just like life itself, the phases of the Moon wax and wane. Planning your life by the Moon's cycles can help you achieve better results—and save you lots of needless heartache.

Chapter 11

The Future Is NOW

Astrology is about more than fixed moments in time; it's a study of cycles—the cycles of the planets, and the cycles of events, cultures, and societies—and how they interweave each other. Every planetary cycle corresponds to cycles of human consciousness and is revealed in everything from political and sociological structures to science, religion, philosophy, myth, music, and art.

A glimpse at this interaction between the heavens and everything on Earth is, appropriately enough, the grand finale, so to speak, of this book. We finish up our exploration of astrology by looking at the big picture, our future.

Welcome to the Year 2000

The year 2000! The talk about what's to come is all over the board. So what's a person to believe? First let's start by considering the change to the millennium number 2 from number 1 and then look at how this change occurs.

We've had almost a thousand years of the number 1 as the millennium number. This number represents courage, me-first attitudes, aggression, competition, and strong desires. This often meant wars, or taking care of number one's needs at the expense of the needs of others. And it frequently meant that whomever was physically strongest was in charge.

The shift to the "2" means that we're moving to a thousand years of learning to live and work in harmony with others, regardless of their point of view. This means learning to cooperate and work together for the betterment of everyone, including the Earth, not just ourselves. When the new millennium gets here, the old ways of living will be out the door!

Ring in the New

With a thousand years of our old ways behind us, what would make people suddenly start working together in harmony? Certainly business as usual won't be what makes us change; we're looking for a very significant change. Enter the year 2000 computer bug—ironically, just in time!

Because many computers and chips in equipment won't recognize the year "00" as 2000, and will think it's 1900 instead, massive computer system failures could occur in the year 2000. There's even the possibility of being without things like power, safe drinking water, gasoline, food, medications, and other normal supplies. Banks might not function normally, planes might not fly, elevators might not work, and telephones could fail. In short, it could be a disaster. And this wouldn't happen in just the United States, it would be a global occurrence.

If such a disaster, or even one that was significantly less drastic, did occur, people would be forced to pull together and learn to solve the major problems facing us by working together. Instead of solving this through violent means, we'd be dependent on the skills and talents of everyone around us to overcome the survival issues of the day. And no matter what your status was before this occurred, you and everyone around you would have the same status in a disaster—that of trying to survive. With Uranus in Aquarius, equality for all people is a goal and this is one way to get it!

What Do the Planets Say?

Could the Year 2000 computer bug actually do that much damage? Yes it could. And does it show up astrologically? The answer is an unqualified yes. Saturn in Taurus represents our established structures, including businesses, all types of governments, and organizations. It will be astrologically challenged by Uranus in Aquarius, which represents established technology that's difficult to change. That sounds like the computer date code problem all right, making it tough on our structures and systems.

This same aspect last occurred in these signs in January 1501, well before Uranus was ever "discovered." Once a planet has been discovered, its energies operate on a much more conscious level, and we now have computers and high technology. In essence, this is the first time this aspect has ever occurred since the discovery of Uranus and the invention of the computer. And it's certainly the first time we've ever encountered this situation with our computers. This aspect will last about two years (on and off) from May 1999 through May 2001.

This same aspect (Saturn in Taurus square to Uranus in Aquarius) becomes involved in a very serious line up with the other planets in May 2000. In fact, eight out of all ten planets are involved in this aspect! What might this mean? It's hard to be sure, but a lot of systems could fail at the same time, and we could have a major economic recession or worse. Could the computer bug cause all that? Yes it could. Will it cause all that? It's hard to know for sure.

It's possible that these same symbols might mean the Earth gets hit by an asteroid, or solar flares strike our power grids and knock out our systems. Or perhaps the aliens really do show up and reveal themselves! (Hopefully they'll help fix our computers if they do!) Uranus in Aquarius also symbolizes aliens of all types and anything that suddenly comes out of the blue, such as an asteroid or solar flare. So there are other possibilities! But the computer bug seems the most likely scenario.

In any event, the essence of this event is that life as we know it will change. It may not be easy at first, but in the long run, it will be for the best. We'll learn to work together to meet everyone's needs, including the Earth's needs, and not just those of some people. Fortunately we'll have all those new ideas, new inventions, and new ways of thinking to help us cope with this. Plus we'll have plenty of heavenly assistance to help us get through this, as you'll soon see. What's important is to change our consciousness from the ways of the "1" to the ways of the "2!"

Astrological High and Low Times

Philosopher-astrologer, E. Alan Meece, author of *Horoscope for a New Millennium*, has plotted "high times" and "low times" for all of human history, and has discovered that high times occur precisely when the three outer planets, Uranus, Neptune, and Pluto, are in what he calls the high signs—Scorpio, Sagittarius, Capricorn, and Aquarius.

High times herald cultural and artistic innovation. On Meece's timelines, the eras during which all three outer planets were in high signs include the late 1400s to early 1500s (Columbus, Michelangelo, da Vinci), the mid-1600s (Rembrandt, the Taj Mahal, Isaac Newton), the 1820s (Beethoven, the British Romantic poets, Hegel)—and now.

In fact, the present time is the "highest" in human history. As Meece says, it "may be the best opportunity in all of history to be super creative, if we open our eyes to the awesome possibilities around us." All three outer planets will be in their "high times" until 2003, and until 2012, both Neptune and Pluto will continue their high times.

What's most compelling about the present positions and relationships of these outer planets is that it's the first time since they've been "discovered" that this has happened (the outer planets in the "high" signs). Meece calls these three planets the "key to human destiny." And with the Year 2000 coming quickly, we'll certainly be able to use this help! If you're reading this book after the year 2000 has come and gone, well, you already know what's happened! Our guess is that cooperation is (was, still is...!) the key to the successful transition to the new millennium.

Welcome to the Future: The Super Renaissance

Once we begin to consider what the cycles and patterns of the past can tell us about where we are now and where we're headed, we can see why "the future is now" is such a popular phrase.

Just as during the last Renaissance, in the 1820's, when humankind began "discovering" the sciences, we now have a unique opportunity to "discover" the unknown. The Super Renaissance points us toward our own untapped potentials, and physicists are in the forefront.

Physicists are exploring how the underlying realities (or inner realities) are enfolded together with our outer or external realities. These are known as the implicate and explicate orders. These theories are trying to tie together the entire universe.

While these physicists chart courses through unknown waters, astrologers know that whenever Uranus and Pluto get together, "business as usual" is out the door. This most recently happened during the 60s, and those of us who re-member that decade can well recall the radical changes that occurred or began during that time.

Written in the Skies

Revolutionary movements always begin during Uranus-Pluto conjunc-tions and then reach their peak at the Uranus-Pluto opposition, a time of conflict, when the new challenges the old.

Here are some examples from history:

Uranus-Pluto Aspects and Revolutions

Date	Uranus-Pluto Aspect	Events
1711	Conjunction	Freemasons, Voltaire's writing
1793	Opposition	Height of French Revolution
1850	Conjunction	Revolutions throughout Europe
		Taiping Rebellion in China

Date	Uranus-Pluto Aspect	Events
1901	Opposition	Boxer Rebellion
		Philippine Revolt against the United States
		Progressivism in the United States
		Bolshevism in Russia
1966	Conjunction	Cultural Revolution, women's movement, Black Power, peace and ecology movements
2047	Opposition	Climax of the "third revolution"?

Source: E. Alan Meece 1975–76

Looking into Our Astrological Crystal Ball

It's time to get out our astrological crystal ball and predict what's in store for the world's future.

First, let's go back to philosopher E. Alan Meece to see what he has to say about the future. For starters, Meece believes unequivocally that the time of big wars is behind us. Oh, there will still be squabbles and revolutions. But, Meece believes, global war is a thing of the past. This is certainly good news.

More good news is that the period of spiritual renewal that began in 1966 will gather still more momentum. Growing numbers of people will accept alternative and holistic healing practices (this is already happening even within the medical profession), and these will be integrated into conventional medicine.

Many astrologers agree that the new millennium will be a time when the many boundaries that have separated people—political borders, ethnic and race problems, and religious and cultural differences—will begin to dissolve. A global community is in our future, a community of people working together to achieve unimagined possibilities.

With Pluto in Sagittarius transforming all of our social structures, there are some major changes in store that will reshape the way we think and act.

We are poised on the cusp of unimagined possibilities for both humans and humanity. And what we do with the potentials and energies that are represented by the planets is up to each one of us.

We can use astrology to achieve some of these unimagined opportunities, and, to that end, this book is only a beginning. But it's a solid beginning, one we hope you'll embrace as the first step toward a millennium filled with wonderful possibilities for us all.

Astrology and the Tarot

Astrology and the Major Arcana Tarot Cards

Those who read the Tarot well have spent years studying the symbolism and meaning of the cards. There are many interpretations, and one is that the 22 Major Arcana cards correlate to the 12 signs and 10 planets of astrology. While it's impossible to reduce the complex symbolism of Tarot to just one interpretation, we've listed the cards and their astrological equivalents, along with a few possible meanings, below, as an example. For more about Tarot, check out *The Complete Idiot's Guide to Tarot and Fortune-Telling* by Arlene Tognetti and our own Lisa Lenard.

Who's Who?

Tarot Card	Astrological Equivalent	Meaning
0 Fool	Aries ♈	Innocence, openness
1 Magician	Mercury ☿	Creative ability
2 High Priestess	Moon ☽	Intuition
3 Empress	Venus ♀	Abundance, fertility
4 Emperor	Mars ♂	Authority, father
5 Hierophant	Taurus ♉	Conformity
6 Lovers	Gemini ♊	Choices in life
7 Chariot	Sagittarius ♐	Victory through adversity
8 Strength	Leo ♌	Fortitude, compassion
9 Hermit	Virgo ♍	Truth
10 Wheel of Fortune	Jupiter ♃	Destiny, luck
11 Justice	Libra ♎	Fairness, honor
12 Hanged Man	Neptune ♆	Sacrifice, release
13 Death	Scorpio ♏	Regeneration
14 Temperance	Cancer ♋	Patience, adaptation
15 Devil	Capricorn ♑	Materialism
16 Tower	Uranus ♅	The unexpected
17 Star	Aquarius ♒	Hope, faith
18 Moon	Pisces/Cancer ♓/♋	Imagination
19 Sun	Leo ♌	Contentment
20 Judgement	Pluto ♇	Awakening
21 World	Saturn/Capricorn ♄/♑	Attainment

Astrology and the Minor Arcana Tarot Suits

The 56 Minor Arcana cards of the Tarot deck are divided into four elements, or suits: Wands, Cups, Swords, and Pentacles. Each suit has 14 cards; Ace through 10, and four separate court cards, to represent the people and events of each suit. Each of the four suits correlates to the signs of the zodiac, the elements, and the energies.

Tarot Suit	Astrological Signs	Element	Energy
Wands	Aries, Leo, Sagittarius	Fire	Yang
Cups	Pisces, Cancer, Scorpio	Water	Yin
Swords	Aquarius, Gemini, Libra	Air	Yang
Pentacles	Taurus, Virgo, Capricorn	Earth	Yin

Appendix B

Glossary

Your **ascendant** is your rising sign, the sign that has just risen over the horizon at the moment of your birth. It represents the "you" that the outside world perceives, as well as personality traits, needs, and your physical characteristics.

Aspect is a technical astrology term. When two planets are in aspect to each other, they are related by one of several geometric angles between them. Aspects can be beneficial or challenging.

Astrology is the study of cycles indicated by planetary movements, and represents your strengths and challenges as well as your soul's purpose.

Your **birth chart** or **horoscope** is a unique map of who you are. Using the date, time, and place of your birth, it shows the positions of the planets in the signs and houses. The odds of anyone else having the same horoscope as you are astronomically small.

A **certified astrologer** is someone who has not only studied astrology, but who also has taken professional tests to become certified. These tests are tough. They usually last at least eight hours, and sometimes go for days.

A **conjunction of planets** means that the two planets appear in the same place in the sky at the same time. It begins a new cycle, a cycle that reflects the planets involved.

Cusps are the beginning of each house. The ascendant, for example, is the beginning of the First House, the house of self, and the next cusp is the beginning of the Second House, etc. The cusps also separate the houses from each other.

Your **descendant** is the cusp of your seventh house, and represents how you channel your energies through partnerships and relationships.

The four **elements** describe the basic qualities of the signs and of life. There are three signs for each element. The fire signs are Aries, Leo, and Sagittarius; the earth signs are Taurus, Virgo, and Capricorn; the air signs are Gemini, Libra, and Aquarius; and the water signs are Cancer, Scorpio, and Pisces.

The **energies** represent whether the energy manifested by a Sun sign is yang/direct and externally oriented or yin/indirect and internally oriented.

Financial astrology studies how and when you can best invest your money, as well as the best companies for you to invest in.

The **houses** are the "where" of astrology. Each of the 12 houses encompasses a specific arena of life and is the stage where the drama of the planets unfolds.

Medical astrology uses your chart to determine the best ways for you to stay healthy and achieve a sense of well-being. It also can be used for diagnosis.

Your **midheaven**, or **MC**, represents your ambition, career, or social role and public image. It's the highest point that the Sun reached on the day of your birth. Your IC is the point on your birth chart that represents your life's foundations and psychological roots. It's found on the exact opposite side of the earth from the midheaven.

Moon phases are the names for the eight parts of the Moon's $29^1/_2$-day cycle. They are: the New Moon, Crescent Moon, First Quarter Moon, Gibbous Moon, Full Moon, Disseminating Moon, Last Quarter Moon, and the Balsamic Moon.

Mundane astrology examines what is happening, not to individuals, but rather to the bigger picture—to society, countries, and cultures.

Mutable signs occur as the season is changing and so are associated with transitions. The mutable signs are Gemini, Virgo, Sagittarius, and Pisces.

Opposite signs, or a polarity, are signs that appear directly across from each other in the zodiac. Taurus and Scorpio are opposites, for example.

Planets are the "what" of astrology. They represent your various energies, including your mental and emotional nature, desires, vitality, soul, will, consciousness, and subconscious, as well as the people in your life. In this book, we include the Sun and Moon, even though they aren't actually planets.

Qualities represent different types of activities and are related to where in a season a sign falls. Cardinal signs begin each season, so they like to begin things; fixed signs, in the middle of each season, are preservers, keeping things as they are; and mutable signs occur as the season is changing, and so are associated with transitions.

Relationship astrology studies people's charts to determine their compatibility or incompatibility.

Planetary **rulers** are in charge of certain signs, and so these planets and signs share certain characteristics.

The **signs of the zodiac** are: Aries, Taurus, Gemini, Cancer, Leo, Virgo, Libra, Scorpio, Sagittarius, Capricorn, Aquarius, and Pisces. All zodiac signs appear in everyone's chart. Signs are the "how" of astrology, and show the needs and styles of the planets, as well as what methods could be used to achieve them.

A **Sun sign** represents the position of the Sun in the heavens at the moment of your birth. When someone asks you what your sign is, he or she is referring to your Sun sign.

Synchronicity is the idea that everything in the universe is interconnected, a pattern of meaningful coincidences, or, as Jung said, everything that is born or occurs at a particular time has the energies of that time!

Vocational astrology studies your potentials in order to determine your career or path.

When the Moon is **void of course**, its energy is spent, and this is a time of gestation, research, or rest. Either nothing will come of decisions made during this time, or there will be unexpected problems that can prevent a successful completion.

A **waning Moon** decreases in light from the Full Moon until the next New Moon.

A **waxing Moon** grows in light from the New Moon to the Full Moon.

The **zodiac** is the name of the elliptic pattern the Earth follows in its annual revolution around the Sun. This path is always the same, and always passes through the same 12 signs.

Index